aus der Reihe:

Innovationen mit Mikrowellen und Licht

**Forschungsberichte aus dem Ferdinand-Braun-Institut,
Leibniz-Institut für Höchstfrequenztechnik**

Band 48

Nikolai Wolff

Wideband GaN Microwave Power Amplifiers
with Class-G Supply Modulation

Herausgeber: Prof. Dr. Günther Tränkle, Prof. Dr.-Ing. Wolfgang Heinrich

Ferdinand-Braun-Institut	Tel.	+49.30.6392-2600
Leibniz-Institut	Fax	+49.30.6392-2602
für Höchstfrequenztechnik (FBH)		
Gustav-Kirchhoff-Straße 4	E-Mail	fbh@fbh-berlin.de
12489 Berlin	Web	www.fbh-berlin.de

Innovations with Microwaves and Light

Research Reports from the Ferdinand-Braun-Institut,
Leibniz-Institut für Höchstfrequenztechnik

Preface of the Editors

Research-based ideas, developments, and concepts are the basis of scientific progress and competitiveness, expanding human knowledge and being expressed technologically as inventions. The resulting innovative products and services eventually find their way into public life.

Accordingly, the *"Research Reports from the Ferdinand-Braun-Institut, Leibniz-Institut für Höchstfrequenztechnik"* series compile the institute's latest research and developments. We would like to make our results broadly accessible and to stimulate further discussions, not least to enable as many of our developments as possible to enhance everyday life.

In this work, efficient class-G supply modulated RF power amplifier systems for future wireless communications have been investigated and developed to worldwide state-of-the-art performance. The first ever thorough analysis of the operation principle of GaN power amplifiers under class-G modulation was performed along with the development of suitable modulator hardware and RF power amplifiers. In addition, the required measurement and linearization system as well as the developed linearization model, able to handle the arising discontinuous non-linearity, are described. World record efficiency and bandwidth results are shown for a discrete level supply modulated system based on these principles.

We wish you an informative and inspiring reading

Prof. Dr. Günther Tränkle
Director

Prof. Dr.-Ing. Wolfgang Heinrich
Deputy Director

The Ferdinand-Braun-Institut

The Ferdinand-Braun-Institut researches electronic and optical components, modules and systems based on compound semiconductors. These devices are key enablers that address the needs of today's society in fields like communications, energy, health and mobility. Specifically, FBH develops light sources from the visible to the ultra-violet spectral range: high-power diode lasers with excellent beam quality, UV light sources and hybrid laser systems. Applications range from medical technology, high-precision metrology and sensors to optical communications in space. In the field of microwaves, FBH develops high-efficiency multi-functional power amplifiers and millimeter wave frontends targeting energy-efficient mobile communications as well as car safety systems. In addition, compact atmospheric microwave plasma sources that operate with economic low-voltage drivers are fabricated for use in a variety of applications, such as the treatment of skin diseases.

The FBH is a competence center for III-V compound semiconductors and has a strong international reputation. FBH competence covers the full range of capabilities, from design to fabrication to device characterization.

In close cooperation with industry, its research results lead to cutting-edge products. The institute also successfully turns innovative product ideas into spin-off companies. Thus, working in strategic partnerships with industry, FBH assures Germany's technological excellence in microwave and optoelectronic research.

Wideband GaN Microwave Power Amplifiers with Class-G Supply Modulation

vorgelegt von
M.Sc.
Nikolai Wolff
geboren in Berlin

von der Fakultät IV – Elektrotechnik und Informatik
der Technischen Universität Berlin
zur Erlangung des akademischen Grades
Doktor der Ingenieurwissenschaften
Dr.-Ing.
genehmigte Dissertation

Promotionsausschuss:
Vorsitzender: Prof. Dr.-Ing. habil. Dietmar Kissinger
Gutachter: Prof. Dr.-Ing. habil. Wolfgang Heinrich
Prof. Dr.-Ing. Dr.-Ing. habil. Robert Weigel
Prof. Dr. Christian Fager

Tag der wissenschaftlichen Aussprache: 21. August 2018

Berlin 2018

Bibliografische Information der Deutschen Nationalbibliothek

Die Deutsche Nationalbibliothek verzeichnet diese Publikation in der
Deutschen Nationalbibliografie; detaillierte bibliographische Daten sind im Internet
über http://dnb.d-nb.de abrufbar.

1. Aufl. - Göttingen: Cuvillier, 2019
  Zugl.: (TU) Berlin, Univ., Diss., 2018

© CUVILLIER VERLAG, Göttingen 2019
  Nonnenstieg 8, 37075 Göttingen
  Telefon: 0551-54724-0
  Telefax: 0551-54724-21
  www.cuvillier.de

Alle Rechte vorbehalten. Ohne ausdrückliche Genehmigung des Verlages ist
es nicht gestattet, das Buch oder Teile daraus auf fotomechanischem Weg
(Fotokopie, Mikrokopie) zu vervielfältigen.
1. Auflage, 2019
Gedruckt auf umweltfreundlichem, säurefreiem Papier aus nachhaltiger Forstwirtschaft.

  ISBN 978-3-7369-9931-2
  eISBN 978-3-7369-8931-3

Acknowledgment

This work was conducted at the Ferdinand-Braun-Institut, Leibniz-Institut für Höchstfrequenztechnik in the III-V Electronics department in the time between August 2014 and February 2018.

I would like to express my deepest gratitude to my supervisors Prof. Dr.-Ing. habil. Wolfgang Heinrich and Dr. Olof Bengtsson. You introduced me into the wonderful world of science and guided my work to ensure good scientific practice.

I also want to thank Sebastian Preis and Sophie Paul, my Ph.D. student colleagues in the RF power lab. You were always there for discussions and with inspiring ideas. Furthermore, I would like to thank my colleagues at the III-V Electronics department for the good working atmosphere and the many social activities outside work.

Abstract

The continuous and rapidly growing demand for mobile communication access led worldwide to a major increase in the number of base stations to provide the sufficient coverage and quality of service. As a consequence, mobile communication networks have become a significant contributor to the worldwide energy consumption. The necessity to save operational cost and the increased energy awareness fueled research on the efficiency optimization of base station transceivers. A close view at the transceiver shows that the RF power amplifiers in the transmitter are dominating the power consumption of today's base stations, with a share between 50% and 80%. In order to cope with the rapidly increasing access bandwidth, broadband operation with multicarrier modulation formats that provide high spectral efficiency is required. Thus, the RF power amplifier must operate energy-efficient as well as highly linear over a wide dynamic range, due to the large peak-to-average power ratio of the modulated signals. Classical RF power amplifiers cannot fulfil these requirements. Several advanced topologies for efficiency improvement of RF power amplifiers have been developed. Modulating the amplifiers supply voltage according to the variation of the envelope signal is one of the most promising concepts. This topology is investigated in this thesis, with an architecture that switches the supply voltage of the power amplifier in discrete levels with a class-G supply modulator.

The thesis addresses comprehensively all aspects of class-G supply modulation. First, the behavior of linear RF power amplifiers and those with reduced conduction angle when operated with supply modulation is analyzed theoretically. Based on the results several prototype designs were realized, to validate the theory and to gain experience on the influence of the various parameters, such as the discrete supply voltage levels, the switching thresholds, and the interface between the RF PA and the class-G supply modulator. This comprised efforts both on improving the RF power amplifiers and developing several class-G supply modulators.

The measurement system for the dynamic characterization of class-G modulated RF amplifiers and the linearization with baseband digital predistortion plays a key role in this work. Accordingly, the system setup, the dynamic range, and the bandwidth requirements for the measurements with digital predistortion are addressed and different dynamic range enhancement techniques are evaluated and implemented. Class-G supply modulated RF power amplifiers based on gallium nitride technology exhibit a strong nonlinear behavior, therefore linearization is required. For this purpose, the linearization with digital predistortion based on behavioral models is optimized for the class-G topology and a novel predistorter model is developed and analyzed.

Finally, the milestone class-G systems developed during this work are presented and discussed. This begins with the design and analysis of the first dynamically operated class-G supply-modulated RF power amplifier system that provides a modulation bandwidth up to 20 MHz. It covers the progress up to a PA module that provides an instantaneous modulation bandwidth of 120 MHz and achieves better performance than state-of-the art continuous supply modulation systems.

Kurzfassung

Der kontinuierlich und rapide steigende Bedarf an mobilem Zugang zu Kommunikationsnetzen führte weltweit zu einem deutlichen Anstieg von installierten Mobilfunk-Basisstationen, um eine flächendeckende Versorgung mit der nötigen Qualität sicherzustellen. Dies hat dazu geführt, dass die mobilen Kommunikationsnetze signifikant zum weltweiten Energieverbrauch beitragen. Die Notwendigkeit zur Einsparung von Betriebskosten und das steigende Bewusstsein im Umgang mit dem Verbrauch von Energie hat dabei Forschungen zur Effizienzsteigerung dieser Systeme in den Mittelpunkt gerückt. Bei einer Analyse des Energieverbrauchs in einer heutigen Mobilfunk-Basisstation wird schnell ersichtlich, dass der HF-Leistungsverstärker dabei den bedeutendsten Anteil beiträgt und zwischen 50% und 80% der Energie verbraucht. Durch die rasch wachsenden Datenraten werden breitbandige Mehrträger-Modulationsformate mit hoher spektraler Effizienz benötigt. Der HF Leistungsverstärker muss dadurch über einen weiten Dynamikbereich sowohl sehr linear als auch effizient arbeiten, da die modulierten Signale ein hohes Verhältnis von Spitzen- zu Mittelwertleistung haben. Klassische HF Leistungsverstärker erfüllen diese Anforderungen nur ungenügend. Aus dieser Problematik heraus wurden verschiedene Verstärkertopologien mit verbesserter power back-off Effizienz entwickelt. Ein vielversprechendes Konzept in diesem Zusammenhang ist die Modulation der Versorgungsspannung des HF Leistungsverstärkers mit der Einhüllenden des modulierten Signals. Ein Sonderfall dieser Topologie mit diskreten Versorgungsspannungsstufen (Klasse-G Modulation der Versorgungsspannung) wird in dieser Arbeit untersucht.

Die Arbeit behandelt alle Aspekte eines Klasse-G-modulierten HF-Leistungsverstärkers. Zu Beginn werden die Eigenschaften von linearen Verstärkern und solchen mit reduziertem Stromleitwinkel für den Betrieb mit variabler Versorgungsspannung theoretisch untersucht. Auf Basis dieser Voruntersuchungen werden dann Prototypen realisiert. Mit Hilfe von Messungen wird so die Validität der Theorie überprüft und der Einfluss der vielzähligen Parameter, wie z.B. die Wahl der diskreten Versorgungsspannungen, die Schwellen für das Umschalten der Versorgungsspannung und die elektrische Verbindung zwischen Klasse-G Modulator und HF Verstärker untersucht. Parallel zur Weiterentwicklung der HF Leistungsverstärker werden Klasse-G-Versorgungsspannungsmodulatoren entwickelt und an die Anforderungen angepasst.

Ein weiterer wichtiger Teil dieser Arbeit befasst sich mit dem Aufbau eines Messplatzes für die dynamische Charakterisierung der Klasse-G-modulierten HF-Leistungsverstärker und der Linearisierung mittels digitaler Vorverzerrung im Basisband. Des Weiteren werden der erforderliche Dynamikumfang für die Linearisierung mittels digitaler Vorverzerrung und verschiedene Konzepte zur Erhöhung des Dynamikumfangs mittels Signalverarbeitung untersucht und implementiert. Auf Galliumnitrid-Technologie basierende Klasse-G-modulierte HF-Leistungsverstärker zeigen im Betrieb ein stark nichtlineares Verhalten. Die Kompensation der Nichtlinearitäten wird mittels einer digitalen Vorverzerrung, die auf Verhaltensmodellen beruht, implementiert und ein neues für Klasse-G-Betrieb optimiertes Modell eingeführt.

Abschließend werden die Meilensteine der in dieser Arbeit entwickelten Klasse-G Systeme zusammengefasst und vorgestellt. Dies beginnt mit dem ersten rudimentären Prototyp, der den dynamischen Klasse-G Betrieb mit Signalen bis 20 MHz Modulationsbandbreite ermöglicht, und endet bei einem System mit einer Modulationsbandbreite von 120 MHz, das den aktuellen Stand der Technik der kontinuierlich versorgungsspannungsmodulierten Systeme erreicht und hinsichtlich der Bandbreite deutlich übertrifft.

Contents

Acknowledgment I

Abstract III

Kurzfassung... V

Contents.. VII

1   Introduction 1

2   Theory of Class-G Supply Modulation 5

   2.1   Supply modulation of linear and reduced conduction angle power amplifiers 6

      2.1.1   Power back-off efficiency with continuously reduced supply voltage 7

      2.1.2   Power back-off efficiency for discretized supply voltage modulation 13

      2.1.3   Quasistatic GaN-HEMT model based simulations with knee I-V effects 15

   2.2   Class-G modulator switching speed requirements..20

   2.3   Efficiency enhancement limits of class-G supply modulation 30

   2.4   Power amplifier linearity under class-G supply modulation 35

      2.4.1   Baseband signal distortions caused by gain and phase variations 36

      2.4.2   Impact of class-G supply modulation on the transducer gain 36

      2.4.3   Quantification of nonlinear distortions in class-G supply modulated PAs 38

   2.5   Conclusions..43

3   RF Power Amplifiers for Supply Modulation..45

   3.1   The RF power GaN-HEMT 45

      3.1.1   The Gallium-Nitride III-V semiconductor properties 45

      3.1.2   Epitaxial and device structure of a GaN-HEMT..46

      3.1.3   Electrical characteristics of the FBH GaN-HEMTs.......................................47

   3.2   Impact of charge-trapping in GaN-HEMTs on RF performance......................51

      3.2.1   Dynamic I-V measurements...52

      3.2.2   Slow compressive gain and its relation to gate-lag...55

      3.2.3   Drain current degradation in relation to the drain-lag....................................56

3.2.4 Conclusions 60

3.3 Design considerations for supply modulation 60

    3.3.1 Supply voltage dependent output impedance matching 61

    3.3.2 Probability distribution optimized design for class-G supply modulation 62

    3.3.3 Bias circuitry design for class-G operation 65

    3.3.4 Stability analysis 68

4 Class-G Supply Modulators 73

    4.1 GaN-HEMT switching stages 73

        4.1.1 GaN-based Schottky diodes 75

    4.2 Galvanically isolated gate drivers 76

        4.2.1 Digital Isolators 78

        4.2.2 Isolated DC/DC converters 79

        4.2.3 Common-mode suppression 81

    4.3 Class-G supply modulator designs 82

        4.3.1 The first generation 82

        4.3.2 The second generation 85

        4.3.3 The third generation 86

5 Measurement Setup and Optimization 89

    5.1 Multiple-input single-output setup for wideband modulated measurements 89

    5.2 Synchronization 90

    5.3 Dynamic range enhancement 91

6 Digital Predistortion and Signal Processing for Class-G Power Amplifier Systems . 95

    6.1 Baseband digital predistortion 95

    6.2 Peak-to-average power reduction 97

    6.3 Iterative learning control 101

    6.4 Behavioral model based digital predistortion 102

        6.4.1 Volterra-based models 102

        6.4.2 Model optimization for class-G operation 104

    6.4.3   Bandwidth requirements 106

  6.5   Predistorter model training and coefficient extraction 107

    6.5.1   Model coefficient extraction 107

    6.5.2   Predistorter training based on iterative learning architecture 108

    6.5.3   Predistorter training based on iterative learning control 109

7   Class-G RF Power Amplifier System Optimization 111

  7.1   State-of-the-art 111

  7.2   Milestone Class-G Systems 112

    7.2.1   40 W RF power amplifier based system operating at 2.65 GHz 112

    7.2.2   65W three-level class-G systems with over 50% PAE at 1.85GHz and 20 MHz instantaneous modulation bandwidth 117

    7.2.3   Discrete-level gate bias and supply modulated PA 121

    7.2.4   79W three-level class-G systems with over 38% PAE at 1.8GHz and 120 MHz instantaneous modulation bandwidth 124

8   Summary and Outlook 129

9   Appendix 131

  9.1   Conduction angles, quiescent and ac current 131

  9.2   Intermodulation distortion 132

10   Symbols and abbreviations 135

11   References 137

12   Publications 145

1 Introduction

The worldwide power consumption of telecommunication networks is rapidly growing due to the steadily increasing demand on broadband internet access. With an estimated annual growth rate of over 10% and an estimated total power consumption of 257 TWh in 2012 [1], telecommunication networks contribute significantly to the worldwide power consumption. In line with this, broadband wireless data access is rapidly developing towards higher bandwidth, with a continuously growing amount of mobile subscriptions and mobile traffic [2]. For the required wireless transmission of data, a modulated radio frequency (RF) signal must be generated and amplified by an RF power amplifier (PA) to provide the output power that is high enough to compensate for the immense path-losses in a wireless transmission link, in which the attenuation scales with the square of the distance [3] - even for optimum free-space conditions. Therefore, an RF PA is needed in each base station transmitter and it is a key component when it comes to system efficiency: The RF PA consumes 50-80% of the total energy and is therefore the most power-hungry part in a base station [4]. The PA must fulfill the linearity requirements to avoid emission outside the specified RF band, since the frequency spectrum is densely utilized, and to allow transmission with low bit-error rates. This suggests operating the PA in a linear regime where it is guaranteed that also the highest power peaks are amplified without driving the PA into compression. The need for high data throughput and a high number of users demands for a structured and efficient utilization of the RF spectrum with modulation schemes that provide high spectral efficiency. In communication standards like long-term-evolution (LTE), which belongs to the 4th generation (4G) wireless networks, and the future 5G technology, orthogonal frequency-division-multiplexing (OFDM) is used for modulating the downlink channel, i.e., the transmission link from the base station to the mobile handset. For OFDM modulated signals the peak-to-average power ratio (PAPR), i.e., the ratio between peak power and average transmitted power, is usually very high [5]. The PAPR increases with the number of modulated subcarriers [6], which makes the design of broadband systems even more challenging. High PAPR requires the operation of the PA in power back-off to maintain linearity. PA architectures like class-A and class-AB [7] are significantly losing efficiency when operated at power back-off. For a class-A this is caused by the fact that the drain-source current is constant while the output power (P_{OUT}) is reduced. Simulations of the drain efficiency vs. power back-off for ideal PAs of different operation classes are shown in Fig. 1.1 (a). The efficiency drops rapidly for all PA classes with conduction angles above 180°, i.e., class-A to -B. For conduction angles above 180° the efficiency increases, but the gain decreases rapidly under power back-off, which is plotted in Fig. 1.1 (b). A good trade-off between gain and back-off efficiency is found in the class-AB range.

Fig. 1.2 shows the simulated drain efficiency at power back-off for different supply voltages and a class-AB PA. The efficiency can be improved in output power back-off by reducing the supply voltage of the PA. This is the key point which most supply modulation techniques are based on: Whenever the PA is operated at an output power below its maximum level, the supply voltage is decreased to achieve an increase in efficiency. In envelope tracking (ET) topologies the supply voltage is modulated with the envelope of the modulated RF signal. In contrast to the Kahn envelope elimination and restoration (EER) approach, the RF input of the PA is still driven with the modulated signal and contains phase- and amplitude information. The supply modulation can be implemented either analog with continuous supply-voltage modulation or with discrete supply voltage levels. In this work, the discrete level supply modulation is referred to as class-G supply modulation. The class-G modulator is in principle a multilevel switch which selects between two or more fixed supply voltages. This thesis investigates theory, design, and operation of such systems.

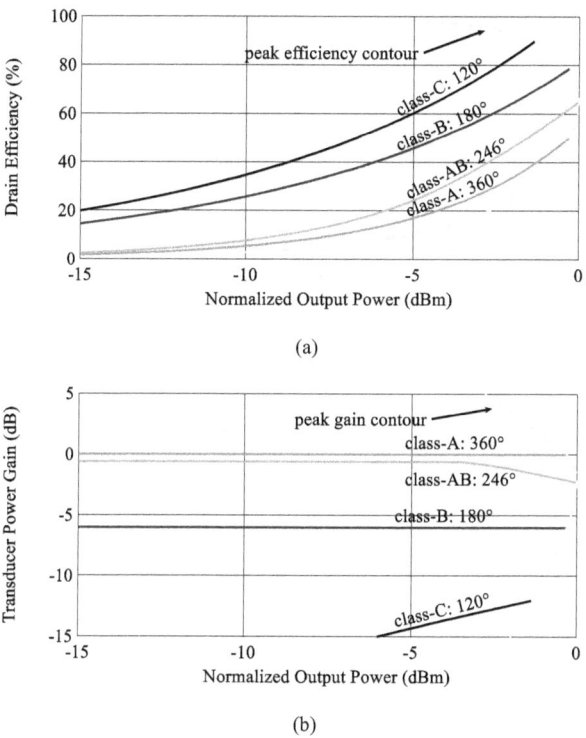

Fig. 1.1: Theoretical (a) drain efficiency and (b) transducer power gain for different conduction angles/amplifier classes vs. output power normalized to the peak output power. The transducer gain is normalized to the gain of a class-A PA.

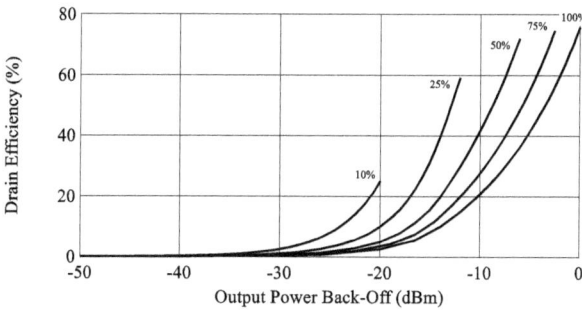

Fig. 1.2: Simulated drain efficiency vs. power back-off of a class-AB PA, when adjusting supply voltage (curve parameter denotes % of maximum supply voltage).

2 Theory of Class-G Supply Modulation

Class-G supply modulation is a discrete-level supply voltage modulation technique, in which the supply voltage of a PA is switched between discrete levels. If the PA is operated with a modulated RF signal, the supply voltage is switched according to the envelope of the modulated signal. Class-G supply modulation is a relatively young concept that was first introduced for low frequency audio applications in 1976 [8]. The adoption of the class-G supply modulation for RF applications was first proposed in [9] and the first RF PA systems with class-G modulation where published in 1995 [10]. It was shown that class-G modulation works well in the RF domain, and that a high efficiency improvement can be achieved. In the initial work on class-G the linearity degradation was not the main focus, since most systems were based on integrated silicon circuits. In general, there were not many publications available on the topic at the beginning of this thesis work in 2014, especially for PA architectures based on gallium nitride (GaN) semiconductors. This has been changed by the achievements presented in this thesis. Nowadays, class-G modulation is a competitive solution which shows performance that compares well with other state-of-the-art efficiency-enhancement techniques.

In the following the concept of class-G supply modulation is discussed in detail. First, the efficiency and transducer gain of a linear PA is analyzed under the conditions of variable power back-off and supply voltage levels, but with a fixed load (R_L). The behavior of the RF PA in relation to these parameters is crucial for the design of highly efficient supply modulated systems and, which is shown in this work, has proven to be a very complex issue. This first design step is usually done based on continuous wave (CW) load-pull measurements or simulations. It is important to know that, due to memory and thermal effects, the CW-based analysis does not exactly fit the behavior of the class-G PA system under dynamic operation, as it was shown in [11]. Nevertheless, the information obtained is useful to understand the effects of the various parameters of the system. Furthermore, the data can be used for simulations to investigate system performance and limitations while considering the effects of the bandwidth and amplitude distribution of the IQ modulated signal. This chapter is divided into three thematic parts. First the efficiency and linearity of a PA at power back-off is evaluated to investigate which amplifier class is best suited for class-G modulation. In the second part the dynamic requirements for the class-G supply modulator are investigated to find out how many supply voltage levels to use and which maximum switching frequency is required for a specific IQ modulation bandwidth and targeted efficiency enhancement. The last part discusses the limitations in efficiency enhancement for the class-G modulation topology.

2.1 Supply modulation of linear and reduced conduction angle power amplifiers

The efficiency of linear and reduced conduction angle PAs, particularly class-A to class-C, depends on the instantaneous output power of the PA. It decreases with lower output power levels, as shown in Fig. 1.2. When a modulated signal with dynamic envelope amplitude is applied to a PA, the average efficiency is degraded since the average output power must be decreased to avoid overdriving the PA at the peak power levels. Therefore, the PAPR of the amplified signal is a very important property from a PA point of view. For a complex-valued signal vector $\underline{x}$, the PAPR (in dB) is defined by:

$$\text{PAPR} = 10 \cdot \log_{10}\left(\max\left(|\underline{x}|^2\right)\right) - 10 \cdot \log_{10}\left(\text{mean}\left(|\underline{x}|^2\right)\right) \qquad (1)$$

The PAPR determines the average power back-off that is required to drive the PA in a linear range, without clipping the maximum signal amplitudes. This is visualized by Fig. 2.1, which shows the time domain envelope- and RF power signals of a class-A PA. The gray shaded area represents the total dissipated energy. It can be concluded, that low envelope power levels significantly contribute to the total dissipated energy.

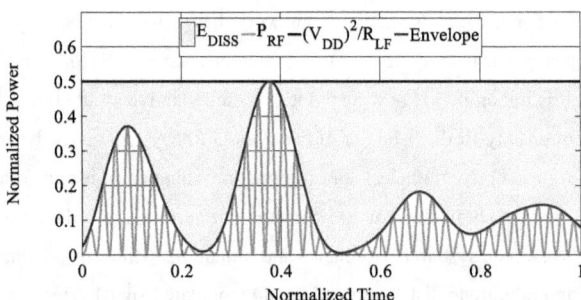

Fig. 2.1: Time domain signals of envelope- and RF power for a constant supply voltage. The dissipated energy is equivalent to the gray shaded area (simplified illustration).

In the following study, the possible performance enhancement of supply modulation and its impact on the PA characteristics are investigated. Therefore, the power back-off behavior of linear power amplifiers is analyzed for reduced supply voltages. Thereby it is considered that R_L is constant (no simultaneous load modulation is applied). The variation of the supply voltage causes a mismatch regarding optimum PAE or P_{OUT}. To investigate this effect, the theory of the reduced conduction angle power amplifier classes [7] is expanded to investigate the power back-off behavior as function of the DC supply voltage levels. For this purpose, the PA is evaluated as a four-port device, two RF ports (p1, p2) and two low frequency (LF) ports (p3, p4), as shown in Fig. 2.2. The RF signal is fed into p1 and the amplified signal is obtained at p2. The supply modulator is connected at the port p3 and provides the DC to LF modulated supply voltage and current. In the first analysis, the LF port p4 is set to a constant bias level, resulting in a simplified three port representation of the PA which is also used in the literature [18]. Later in this chapter the port p4 is also modulated which allows dynamically controlling the quiescent bias point synchronously with the DC supply voltage which can be beneficial for some PA classes.

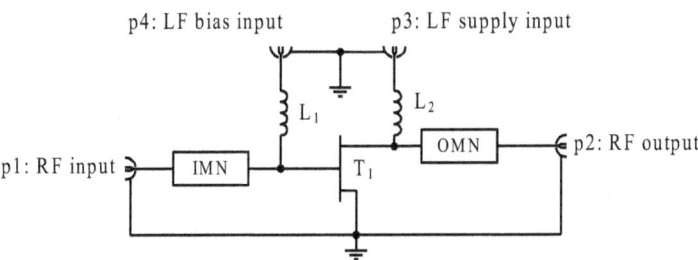

Fig. 2.2: Schematic of the supply modulated PA ports. L_1 and L_2 are RF-chokes, IMN and OMN the input- and output matching networks.

The following part is divided into four subsections: First the reduced conduction angle theory is introduced for supply modulated PAs, based on idealized conditions. Thereby the behavior of the different amplifier classes at power back-off with reduced supply voltage is investigated and the suitability for supply modulation is discussed. In the second part, the influence of discretized supply voltage levels, which represents the case of class-G supply modulation, is investigated. The third part addresses the knee I-V effects based on a quasi-static GaN-HEMT model and compares the result to the theoretically derived values. In the last part the linearity is considered, and the influence of supply modulation is discussed for continuous- and class-G supply modulation.

2.1.1 Power back-off efficiency with continuously reduced supply voltage

In continuous supply modulation the supply voltage of the PA (LF port p3) is adjusted with the envelope amplitude as shown in Fig. 2.3. The comparison to the constant supply voltage case shown in Fig. 2.1 reveals that the area of dissipated energy is reduced significantly.

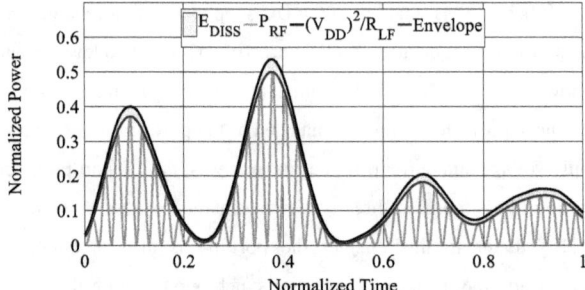

Fig. 2.3: Time domain signals of envelope- and RF power for a continuously modulated supply voltage (simplified illustration).

The analysis is based on an idealized model, where the saturated drain-source current is linearly dependent on the gate-source voltage. The load impedances are all set to be resistive. The drain-source current and -voltage are normalized to their maximum value (I_{DS_MAX}) and V_{DS_MAX}, respectively. In Fig. 2.4 (a) the load-line for a class-A PA is shown for operation with a resistive load and a normalized DC supply voltage (V_{DS_DC}) of 0.5. The conduction angle (α) of the drain-source current is 360°, which makes the drain-source voltage $v_{DS}(t)$ linearly dependent on the drain-source current $i_{DS}(t)$. In this case the PA operates linearly and the load line slope R_{LL} is constant (2) and identical to the load resistance R_L (3):

$$\frac{dR_{LL}}{dt} = \frac{d}{dt}\frac{v_{DS}(t)}{i_{DS}(t)} = 0 \quad , \quad \alpha \geq 360 \qquad (2)$$

$$R_L = R_{LL} \quad , \quad \alpha \geq 360 \qquad (3)$$

For lower conduction angles, the drain-source current is clipped at a level of zero to avoid negative current values. This causes the generation of harmonics. In the reduced conduction angle theory, the fundamental is terminated by a fixed resistance (R_{L1}) and all other harmonics are terminated by a short [7]. Therefore, the amplitude of the AC output voltage ($\hat{v}_{DS\_AC}$) depends only on the amplitude of the fundamental drain-source current ($\hat{i}_{DS\_AC1}$) and R_{L1} (4). This causes the load-line slope to differ from R_{L1} if other harmonics are present (5).

2 Theory of Class-G Supply Modulation

$$\hat{v}_{DS\_AC} = \hat{i}_{DS\_AC1} \cdot R_{L1} \quad (4)$$

$$R_L \neq R_{LL} \quad , \quad \alpha < 360 \quad (5)$$

When supply modulation is applied, the load-line is shifted horizontally, since R_L is constant and the quiescent drain-source current (I_{DSQ}) is independent of V_{DS_DC}. The shift of the load-line and the quiescent bias points with supply voltage is shown in Fig. 2.4 (b) for the class-A case.

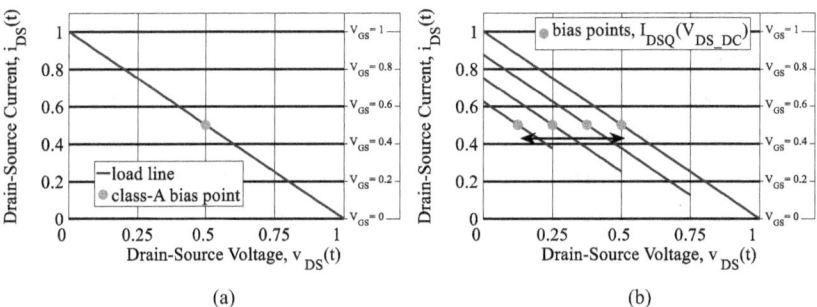

Fig. 2.4: Idealized transistor DC output characteristics with (a) class-A load-line and (b) load-line shift with DC supply voltage reduction.

For the class-A condition shown it is observed that the drain-source current is not excited over its full range and the current AC/DC ratio is reduced. This is caused by the fixed load impedance and the reduced supply voltage and is also valid for other PA classes. With the definition of $v_{DS}(t)$ in (6) the maximum value $\hat{i}_{DS\_AC1}$ can be calculated, based on two conditions. First (7) must be true to avoid negative values of $v_{DS}(t)$ and second (8) must be fulfilled to ensure that $v_{DS}(t)$ does not exceed V_{DS_MAX}. For maximum output power, V_{DS_DC} must be operated in the range from 0 to 0.5, therefore, (8) is not a limitation during operation with reduced V_{DS_DC}.

$$v_{DS}(t) = V_{DS\_DC} - \hat{i}_{DS\_AC1} \cdot \cos(\omega_1 t) \cdot R_{L1} \quad (6)$$

$$\hat{i}_{DS\_AC1}(V_{DS\_DC}) \leq \frac{V_{DS\_DC}}{R_{L1}} \quad , \quad \frac{1}{2} \geq V_{DS\_DC} \quad (7)$$

2 Theory of Class-G Supply Modulation

$$\hat{i}_{DS\_AC1}(V_{DS\_DC}) \leq \frac{1-V_{DS\_DC}}{R_{L1}} \quad , \quad \frac{1}{2} \leq V_{DS\_DC} \tag{8}$$

The limitation of $\hat{i}_{DS\_AC1}$ causes several effects in the supply modulated PA: The maximum output power (P_{OUT_MAX}) becomes dependent on the supply voltage as defined in (9). It scales quadratically with the supply voltage, resulting in a V_{DS_DC} dependent reduction of the maximum output power (P_{OUT_BO}) with a decay of −20 dB/dec (10). Additionally, the efficiency of the PA classes with positive quiescent current ($I_{DSQ} > 0$ A; class-AB to class-A) reduces, since the DC supply current (I_{DS_DC}) does not scale linearly with $\hat{i}_{DS\_AC1}$ (derivation of I_{DS_DC} and $\hat{i}_{DS\_AC1}$ in appendix 9.1). This results in a V_{DS_DC} dependent drop of the DC power consumption at an output power back-off level (P_{DC_BO}) (11) of less than −20 dB/dec. The worst case is a class-A PA, where P_{DC_BO} decreases with only −10 dB/dec, since I_{DS_DC} is constant, independent of V_{DS_DC} ($I_{DS\_DC} = I_{DSQ}$). A possible solution for the class-A case is the modulation of the gate-source bias port (p4) to reduce I_{DSQ} simultaneously with V_{DS_DC}, which is discussed in Chapter 2.1.3. By combining (10) and (11) the drain efficiency at power back-off (η_{D_BO}) in dependency of the peak drain efficiency (η_{D_MAX}), i.e., η_D at maximum supply voltage and output power, is derived in (12). The DC to LF impedance at power back-off (Z_{LF_BO}), seen at port p3, is seen by the supply modulator and, therefore, an important parameter for the design of modulators. The impedance is defined by the fraction of V_{DS_DC} and the current I_{DS_DC} (13). Due to the dependency between V_{DS_DC} and P_{OUT_BO} in (10), Z_{LF_BO} is linearly dependent on the back-off drain efficiency η_{D_BO}.

$$\begin{aligned} P_{OUT\_MAX}(V_{DS\_DC}) &= \frac{\hat{i}_{DS\_AC1}(V_{DS\_DC})^2 \cdot R_{L1}}{2} \\ &= \frac{V_{DS\_DC}^2}{2 \cdot Z_{L1}} \end{aligned} \tag{9}$$

$$\begin{aligned} P_{OUT\_BO}(V_{DS\_DC}) &= 10 \cdot \log_{10}\left(\frac{P_{OUT\_MAX}(V_{DS\_DC})}{P_{OUT\_MAX}(1)}\right) \\ &= 20 \cdot \log_{10}(V_{DS\_DC}) \quad (\text{dB}) \end{aligned} \tag{10}$$

$$P_{DC\_BO}(V_{DS\_DC}) = 10 \cdot \log_{10}\left(\frac{I_{DS\_DC}(V_{DS\_DC})}{I_{DS\_DC}(1)}\right) + \log_{10}(V_{DS\_DC}) \quad (\text{dB}) \tag{11}$$

$$\eta_{D\_BO}(V_{DS\_DC}) = \eta_{D\_MAX} \cdot 10^{\left(\frac{P_{OUT\_BO}(V_{DS\_DC}) - P_{DC\_BO}(V_{DS\_DC})}{10}\right)}$$

$$= \eta_{D\_MAX} \cdot \frac{V_{DS\_DC} \cdot I_{DS\_DC}(1)}{I_{DS\_DC}(V_{DS\_DC})}$$

(12)

$$Z_{LF\_BO}(V_{DS\_DC}) = \frac{V_{DS\_DC}}{I_{DS\_DC}(V_{DS\_DC})}$$

$$= k \cdot \eta_{D\_BO}(V_{DS\_DC})$$

(13)

Fig. 2.5 shows the I_{DS} conduction angle as function of the V_{DS_DC} for selected PA classes. The conduction angle for class-A and class-B is constant over the full supply voltage range. For class-C the conduction angle is reduced with the supply voltage, having the effect that the PA is driven deeper into class-C. The conduction angle of the class-AB region drifts towards class-A, depending on the conduction angle at full supply voltage.

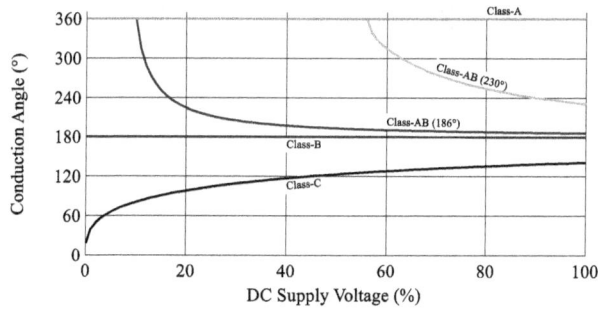

Fig. 2.5: Influence of the supply voltage reduction on the I_{DS} conduction angle for different PA classes.

The horizontal load-line shift shown in Fig. 2.4 (b) is valid in case of a constant conduction angle, i.e., class-A and class-B. For class-AB and class-C the load-line is shifted and additionally the slope changes. This is caused by the fundamental of the drain-source current, $\hat{i}_{DS\_AC1}$, which does not scale linearly with the supply voltage. The load-line slope vs. the supply voltage is shown in Fig. 2.6 for different PA classes. For the class-AB condition the load-line slope is converging towards the resistance of the fundamental load, when V_{DS_DC} is reduced. The calculated drain efficiency as function of the supply-voltage is shown in Fig. 2.7. For class-A, a linear decrease of efficiency with supply-voltage back-off is seen. The class-B case holds a constant efficiency level. For the supply modulator the impedance of the LF supply port of the PA (p3) is very important for the design of filters if used. If the impedance varies with the supply voltage, the filter characteristics will change as well. To evaluate the impedance at p3, I_{DS_DC} (shown in Fig. 2.8) and the supply voltage are used to calculate the impedance is as shown in Fig. 2.9. For class-B the impedance seen by the supply modulator is constant over the supply voltage. For class-A the strongest variation is observed, since the DC current is constant due to the high quiescent current. Therefore, class-B to deep class-AB seem to be viable candidates as bias conditions for supply modulated power amplifiers. Comparing Fig. 2.9 to Fig. 2.7 shows that the drain efficiency and the LF input impedance are linearly dependent, as defined by (13).

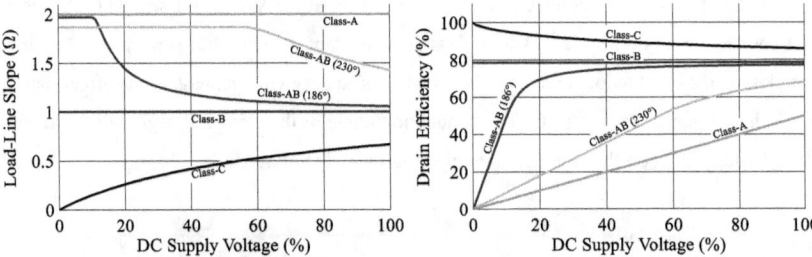

Fig. 2.6: Load-line slope for different conduction angles as function of the DC supply voltage.

Fig. 2.7: Drain efficiency for different PA classes vs. DC supply voltage.

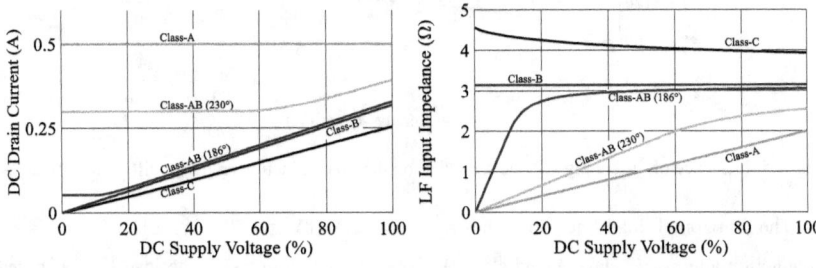

Fig. 2.8: DC value of the drain-source current as function of the DC supply voltage.

Fig. 2.9: Input impedance seen at the LF drain supply port (p3) as function of the DC supply voltage.

In Fig. 2.10 the normalized power gain (referenced to the gain of class-A) is shown. In class-C the gain decreases rapidly with reduced supply voltage, which makes it impracticable for supply modulation. Class-B shows a constant gain 6 dB below the class-A case. This is a significant drawback, since every dB in gain is important in a PA system. The lower gain may not affect the PAE of the main PA significantly, but it requires a preamplifier or a multistage design, depending on the requirements and the technology used. The relationship between

P_{OUT_MAX} and the V_{DS} is shown in Fig. 2.11, according to the definition in (9). The PA class is not influencing the maximum output power at supply voltage back-up. Finally, the definition of the optimum PA class will be based on the statistics of the amplified modulated signal, especially the PAPR. Factors like voltage dependent output capacitances of the transistor [22], charge trapping, knee I-V effects and thermal heating will cause the design to diverge from the ideal theory presented and must be accounted for individually in a PA design.

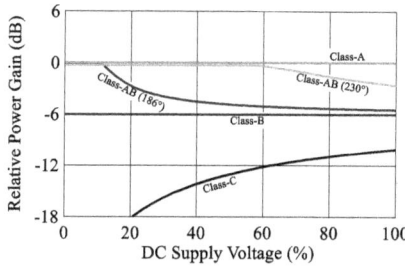

Fig. 2.10: Relative power gain for different PA classes at maximum output power as function of the DC supply voltage.

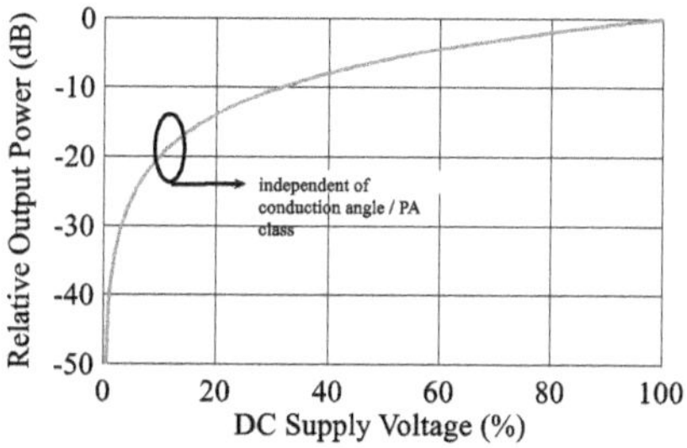

Fig. 2.11: Maximum output power normalized to the power at 100% drain-source voltage for different power amplifier classes / conduction angles.

2.1.2 Power back-off efficiency for discretized supply voltage modulation

The back-off behavior derived in the previous subsection shows the PA behavior for different PA classes when operated at supply voltage back-off. Thereby, the input signal power is adjusted to achieve the maximum output power for the specific supply voltage, resulting in an output power dependent function for the supply voltage setup shown in Fig. 2.11. In class-G operation, only discrete supply voltage levels are available. Fig. 2.12 shows the time domain signals of the envelope- and RF power and the corresponding supply voltage for a three-level class-G modulation.

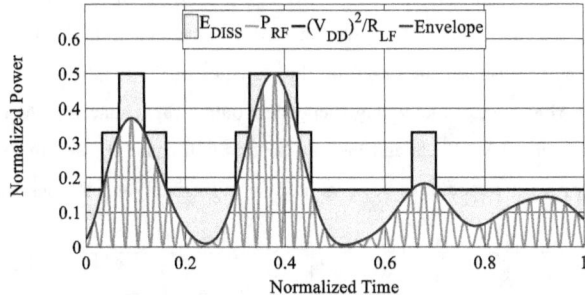

Fig. 2.12: Time domain signals of envelope- and RF power for class-G supply voltage modulation (simplified illustration).

The switching of the supply voltage between the discrete levels causes discontinuities in all supply voltage dependent figures, i.e., the efficiency, DC power consumption, and LF impedance. For the following analysis the supply voltage is modulated with three levels located at 50%, 75% and 100% of the normalized supply voltage as shown in Fig. 2.13. The LF input impedance as function of the normalized output power is plotted in Fig. 2.14. The comparison to Fig. 2.9 shows that the behavior under power back-off significantly changed due to the discretization of the supply voltage. This is on one hand caused by the abrupt changes of the supply voltage and on the other hand by the constant supply voltage levels. Since the LF impedance in combination with a RF-choke represents the load connected to the supply modulator, its behavior is of high importance and needs to be considered carefully in the design of the RF-choke and the dimensioning of the modulator switching stage. This topic is addressed in Chapter 3.3.3. The drain efficiency shown in Fig. 2.15 and the corresponding DC power consumption in Fig. 2.16 are both affected by the discretization of the supply voltage. The back-off efficiency improvement is reduced in the intervals with constant supply voltage, resulting in a supply voltage level dependent efficiency improvement for class-G supply modulation.

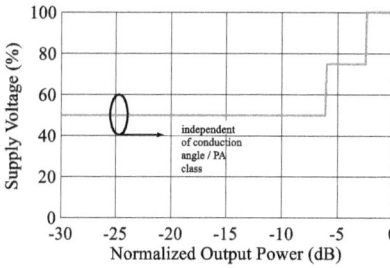

Fig. 2.13: Supply voltage level vs. normalized output power.

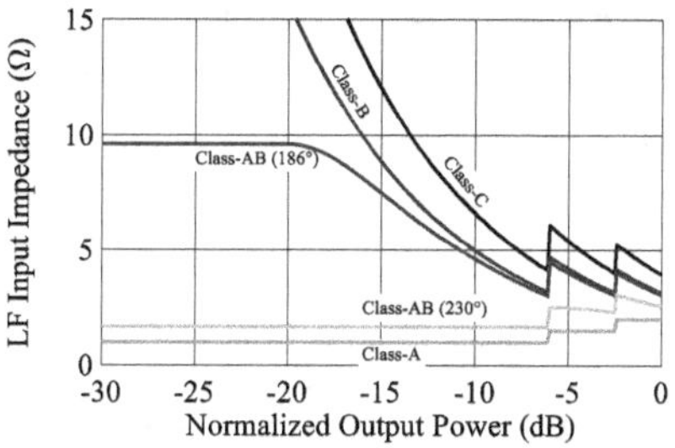

Fig. 2.14: LF input impedance seen at the drain bias interface vs. normalized output power for different conduction angles.

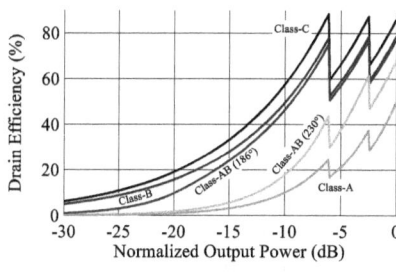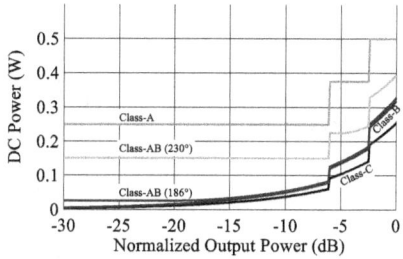

Fig. 2.15: Drain efficiency vs. normalized output power for different conduction angles.

Fig. 2.16: DC power consumption vs. normalized output power for different conduction angles.

2.1.3 Quasistatic GaN-HEMT model based simulations with knee I-V effects

For the analysis of the multiport PA in a realistic environment, a transistor model is used. The model is based on a packaged GaN-HEMT fabricated at the FBH. The transistor has 0.5 µm gate length and a total gate width of 16 mm. It delivers a maximum RF output power of ~80 W at 2 GHz at 40 V supply voltage. This transistor is used in most of the implemented systems presented in Chapter 7 and proved to be very robust and efficient. More details on the technology and the device are presented in Chapter 3.1. The dataset used for the following analysis is based on simulations using the Chalmers model proposed by Angelov et al. [19]. The DC- and thermal characteristics are extracted and applied to the reduced conduction angle power amplifier theory, including the effect of the knee I-V region. The focus is on the qualitative behavior, since details are related to a specific device only and may not have a general importance. The DC characteristics are presented in Fig. 2.17 (a) for the full I-V characteristics and in (b) for the knee I-V region. For supply modulated PAs, the knee I-V region becomes more significant, since its influence on efficiency is increased with reduced V_{DS}. As seen in (b), V_{DS} must be larger than zero for a positive I_{DS}, which limits the maximum efficiency.

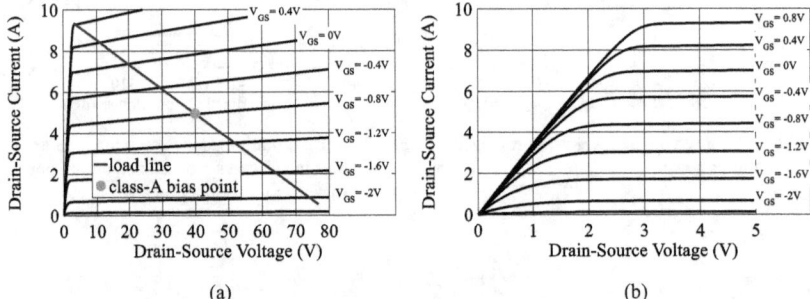

Fig. 2.17: Full DC characteristics with an idealized class-A load-line (a) and knee I-V region (b) of an exemplary RF GaN-HEMT used for class-G supply modulated PAs. Thermal self-heating is not simulated.

The shift of the load line with supply modulation is shown in Fig. 2.18 (a) for a fixed gate-source bias voltage and in (b) for an adaptive bias voltage (applied at port p4, Fig. 2.2). A comparison of Fig. 2.18 (a) with the idealized case Fig. 2.4 (b) shows that the load line is shifted horizontally, but I_{DSQ} exhibits only a weak dependence on V_{DS_DC}. Besides that, the knee I-V voltage is limiting the AC output voltage swing. The modulation of the fourth port shown in Fig. 2.18 (b) reveals some advantages over the three-port implementation shown in (a): First, the reduction of I_{DSQ} reduces the dissipated DC power and second, the impact of the knee I-V region on the possible output voltage swing is reduced. This is verified by the analysis of the amplitude ratio of AC- and the DC drain-source supply voltage ($V_{DS\_AC\_REL}$) shown in Fig. 2.19. With the adaptive biasing, the ratio is kept constant over the full DC supply voltage range.

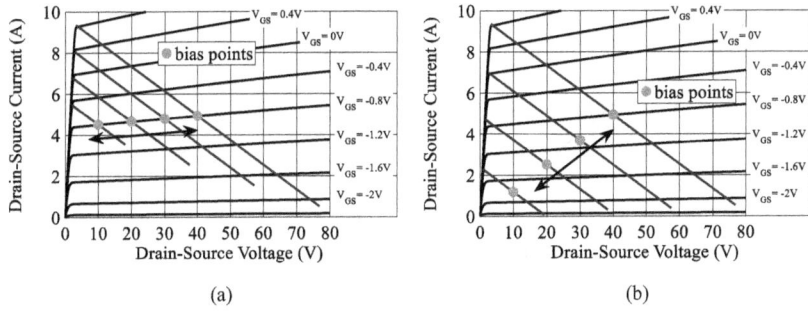

Fig. 2.18: Horizontal shift of the idealized class-A load-line for reduced supply voltages with fixed I_{DSQ} (a) and with combined gate-bias modulation at p4 (b).

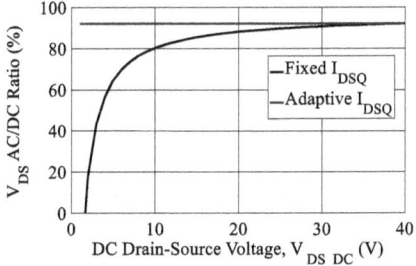

Fig. 2.19: Impact of the knee I-V region on the ratio of AC amplitude and DC supply voltage with fixed quiescent drain-source current and adaptive biasing

The class-A load lines shown in Fig. 2.18 are idealized load lines with constant slope and the PA is not driven into the knee I-V region. The load lines extracted from simulations are shown in Fig. 2.20 (a) for different bias conditions at $V_{DS\_DC} = 40$ V and for a class-A biasing and different V_{DS_DC} in (b). The input power drive is adjusted to achieve $V_{AC\_REL} = 90\%$ to avoid driving the PA into the knee I-V region. Comparing the idealized load line shown in Fig. 2.18 (a) to the simulations in Fig. 2.20 (b) reveals that harmonics are generated since the load line slope is not constant. For reduced supply voltages, an increased impact of the knee I-V region on the possible output voltage swing is observed.

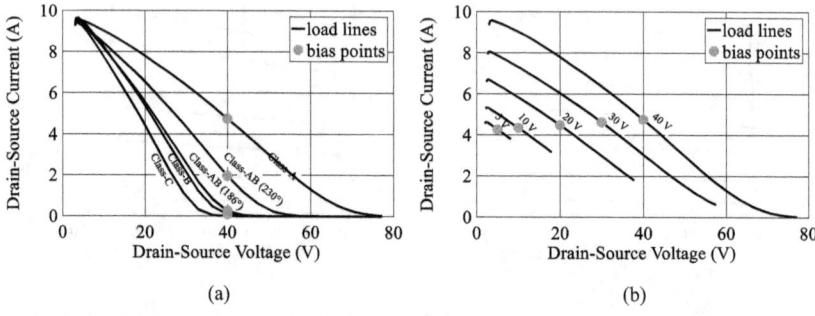

Fig. 2.20: Simulated load-lines for (a) different bias points and fixed V_{DS} and (b) for a class-A condition at different V_{DS}. $V_{AC\_REL} = 90\%$.

The simulation results based on the GaN-HEMT model for the different amplifier classes are shown in the following. The maximum supply voltage level is set to $V_{DS} = 40$ V. Fig. 2.21 shows the drain efficiency as function of V_{DS}. The comparison to the theoretical PA classes (Fig. 2.7) shows a large deviation for low conduction angles (class-C and class-B) for low V_{DS}. The efficiency at the maximum supply voltage shows a slight degradation for the reduced conduction angle classes. For class-A to class-AB the deviation is less significant due to the inherently low efficiency of these PA classes. I_{DS} is shown in Fig. 2.22 and provides more information on the behavior at low supply voltages. The impact of the knee I-V for supply voltages below 5 V is clearly seen in the class-A and class-AB condition, where the current is drastically reduced due to the on resistance (R_{ON}) of the GaN-HEMT. The LF input impedance and the power gain are plotted in Fig. 2.23 and Fig. 2.24, respectively. They are also affected by the knee I-V characteristics. Besides the influence of the knee I-V region, a larger power gain deviation is observed for deep class-AB and class-B biasing. The V_{DS} dependent maximum output power is shown in Fig. 2.25. For the drain efficiency and the LF input impedance an interesting behavior is seen: For the idealized case with continuous supply modulation it was seen that both curves are linearly dependent and scaled by a fixed factor. For the simulations based on the GaN-HEMT model this behavior disappears. The explanation for this behavior is found in the back-off behavior of the maximum output power as function of V_{DS}, which is not constantly decreasing with -20 dB/dec as derived theoretically. This can be verified in the semi-logarithmic representation of the V_{DS} dependent maximum output power for the theoretical- and simulation-based results shown in Fig. 2.26. For levels below 20 V the deviation increases rapidly.

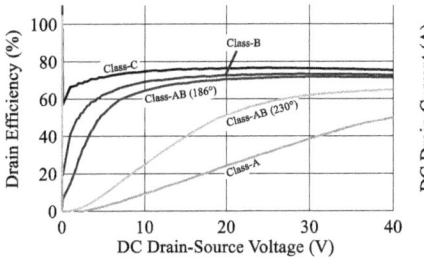

Fig. 2.21: Simulated drain efficiency for different amplifier classes as function of the DC supply voltage.

Fig. 2.22: Simulated DC drain current (I_{DS}) as function of the DC supply voltage.

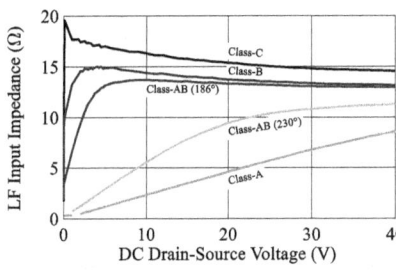
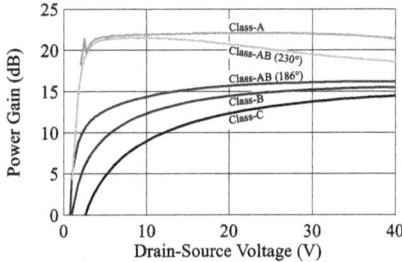

Fig. 2.23: Simulated LF input impedance seen at p3 as function of the DC supply voltage.

Fig. 2.24: Simulated power gain for different amplifier classes as function of the DC supply voltage.

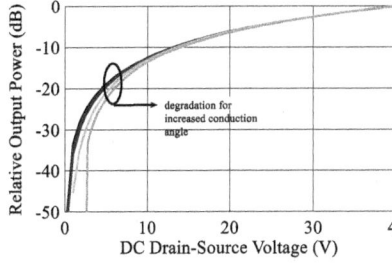
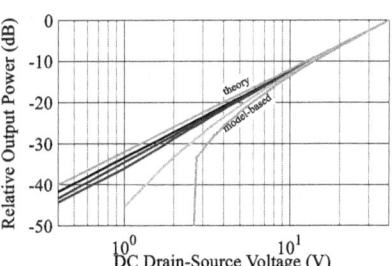

Fig. 2.25: Simulated maximum relative output power as function of the DC supply voltage.

Fig. 2.26: Comparison of theoretical and simulated maximum relative output power as function of the DC supply voltage.

The power-added efficiency (PAE) and G_T are calculated for several fixed supply voltage levels and a fixed quiescent bias current of 600 mA. The simulation results are shown in Fig. 2.27. Self-heating effects are not included in the simulations. For low supply voltages a strong impact of the knee I-V region is visible. For supply modulated systems this is a limiting boundary condition for the lower supply voltage level.

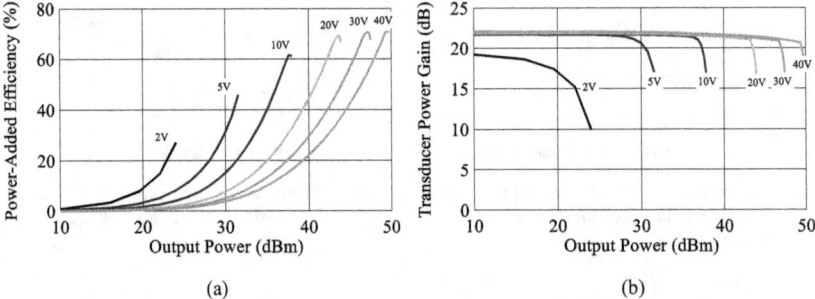

Fig. 2.27: Simulated of (a) PAE and (b) G_T vs. output power for different supply voltages in a class-AB bias point (600 mA quiescent drain current). Harmonics are shorted and fundamental matched to R_{L1} = 8 Ω.

2.2 Class-G modulator switching speed requirements

The previous chapter investigated the PA characteristics at reduced supply voltages. In modulated operation the signal amplitudes are distributed depending on the modulation format. Therefore, the calculation of the performance under modulated operation requires the specification of a modulated signal. In wireless communication the baseband information is modulated on an RF carrier. The spectral efficiency of a modulation format is defined as the ratio of data rate to modulation bandwidth. For optimum utilization of the usable RF spectrum, the spectral efficiency must be as high as possible. Therefore, complex-valued baseband signals, i.e., IQ-signals, are used to fully utilize the lower and upper sideband. A widespread modulation scheme that allows high spectral efficiency and the possibility to handle frequency selective distortions is the orthogonal frequency division multiplexing (OFDM). It allows the modulation of multiple carriers in the frequency domain with arbitrary IQ modulation formats, e.g., QAM. In mobile communication systems OFDM is widely used in downlink channels [23], [24] and is therefore used in this work to generate the reference test signals.

In supply modulated PA systems, the modulator must track the envelope amplitude of the modulated signal. The required envelope signal is independent of the RF carrier and directly available from the baseband IQ signal. The instantaneous envelope $v_{ENV}(t)$ of a complex-valued baseband signal $x_{BB}(t)$ is defined as:

$$v_{ENV}(t) = |x_{BB}(t)|$$
$$= \sqrt{x_I(t)^2 + x_Q(t)^2} \qquad (14)$$

A comparison of the IQ modulation bandwidth and the envelope bandwidth is presented in Fig. 2.28 for an OFDM-modulated signal with 20 MHz modulation bandwidth. Due to the non-linear function of the square root and the power of two in (14), the bandwidth of the envelope signal is expanded to infinity if both signals, in-phase $x_I(t)$ and quadrature $x_Q(t)$, are modulated. This makes it impossible for supply modulators to perfectly track the envelope amplitude in continuous supply modulated systems, but it is sufficient for a continuous supply modulated system to track a bandwidth three to seven times higher than the IQ modulation bandwidth [25], [26]. The efficiency improvement decreases if the bandwidth is further reduced, since a DC offset voltage must be applied to the low-pass filtered envelope signal to ensure that the amplitude does not drop below the original envelope amplitude. Values below the targeted level cause saturation of the PA and degrade the linearity. Furthermore, the low-pass filtering causes an overshoot of the supply voltage and thus may cause temporary operation outside the PA safe operating area. The impact of low-pass filtering on the signal $v_{ENV}(t)$ is shown in Fig. 2.29, where the unfiltered envelope is compared to an ideal low-pass filtered version of (a) 20 MHz and (b) 60 MHz. With the narrow filter bandwidth (a) the amplitude cannot follow the targeted envelope voltage accurately, which requires a higher DC offset. With the wider filter bandwidth in (b) the required DC offset is much lower, and the envelope is tracked more accurately. As a result, the possible efficiency enhancement is higher than in case (a).

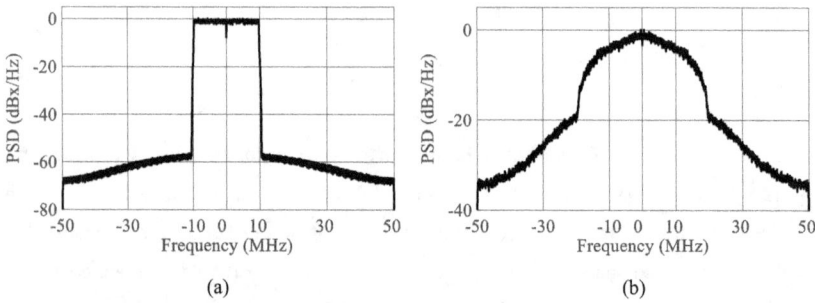

Fig. 2.28: Amplitude power spectral density of (a) an IQ modulated multicarrier baseband signal and (b) its envelope. (An averaging filter is applied in the frequency domain.)

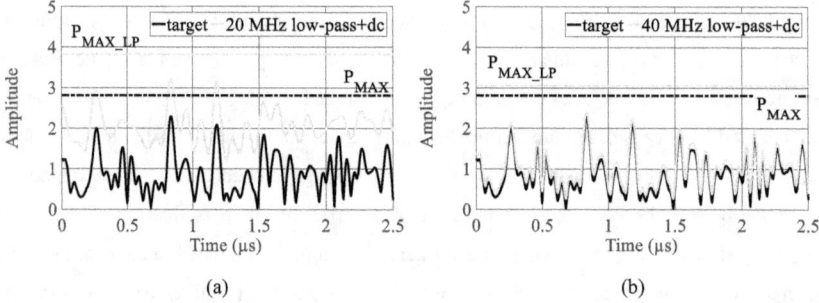

Fig. 2.29: Time domain representation of the low-pass filtered envelope of a 20 MHz OFDM signal, for an ideal filter of (a) 20 MHz and (b) 60 MHz cut-off frequency. A DC offset is applied to the low-pass signal to ensure that the amplitude is always equal or higher than the unfiltered signal. Also, the overall peak amplitude of the entire signal is plotted (denoted by P_{MAX_LP} for the low-pass filtered signal and by P_{MAX} for the original signal, respectively).

Due to the supply voltage discretization in class-G supply modulation, the modulator cannot track the envelope signal accurately. It is therefore accepted that the modulator output signal differs from the envelope. For PAs based on GaN-HEMT technology, nonlinearities are introduced by the supply-modulation since the gain of the PA depends on the supply voltage. With the high computational power available nowadays it is possible to correct the nonlinearities using digital predistortion techniques (DPD), which is discussed in Chapter 6. DPD linearization is only possible, if it is ensured that the supply voltage of the PA is always high enough to avoid overdrive. Compared to continuous supply modulation class-G supply modulation has the advantage that if the envelope dynamics would require the modulator to switch faster than its hardware limits, the control software can skip short pulses and keep a higher supply voltage level instead. Therefore, one does not need a low-pass filter that may cause a supply voltage overshoot. An example for a two-level class-G system is given by

Fig. 2.30 for a fast class-G modulator that tracks all envelope peaks and in Fig. 2.31 for a modulator with an increased minimum pulse width that results in a pulse-skip operation. In both cases the supply voltage is always high enough to avoid driving the PA into saturation. It is obvious that the pulse-skip modulation achieves less efficiency improvement since the area of dissipated energy, E_{DISS}, is increased.

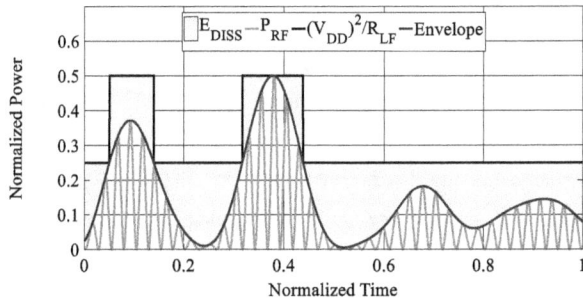

Fig. 2.30: Supply waveform, envelope and RF signal against time for fast two-level class-G modulation.

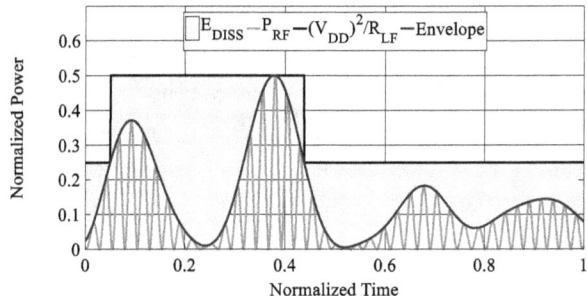

Fig. 2.31: Supply waveform, envelope and RF signal against time for a two-level class-G modulation with increased minimum pulse width, maintaining signal integrity.

The relationship between the IQ modulation bandwidth and the switching speed limitations of the modulator is investigated in the following in detail. The subject turns out to be very complex, especially when the class-G system has more than two supply voltage levels. The results are based on the study in [27]. The following analysis assumes that the linearity is restored using DPD. This assumption is required to ensure that the amplitude probability density function (PDF) of the normalized output signal is equal to the test signal PDF. An important specification of a class-G modulator is the duration of the shortest supply voltage pulses t_{P_MIN} it can deliver to the PA. Based on the definition of t_{P_MIN} the maximum toggle frequency f_{SW_MAX} is derived:

$$f_{SW\_MAX} = \frac{1}{2 \cdot t_{P\_MIN}} \qquad (15)$$

It defines the maximum frequency at which the modulator can switch for a 50% duty-cycle signal. It is used in the following to define the switching speed of a class-G modulator and to define a relation between the IQ modulation bandwidth and the modulator switching speed. It must be noted, that the power spectrum of the modulator output signal has a much higher bandwidth than f_{SW_MAX}, since the modulator generates almost rectangular pulses which contain higher-order harmonics. For the analysis of the relationship between IQ modulation bandwidth and modulator performance, we define the relative switching frequency

$$f_{REL\_G} = \frac{B_{IQ}}{f_{SW\_MAX}} \qquad (16)$$

where B_{IQ} is the IQ modulation bandwidth. With the definition of f_{REL_G} the analysis of the modulator switching speed will be independent of the IQ modulation bandwidth.

Since each modulation format has its own characteristic PDF of the signal power (which also defines the signal PAPR) the following analysis represents only modulation formats based on OFDM accurately. For this analysis an OFDM modulated signal with 9 dB PAPR is used. The modulation bandwidth is 20% of the sampling rate, i.e., 100 MHz IQ modulation bandwidth requires a sampling rate of 500 MS/s. The PDF and the cumulative distribution function (CDF) of the test signal are shown in Fig. 2.32 and Fig. 2.33, respectively.

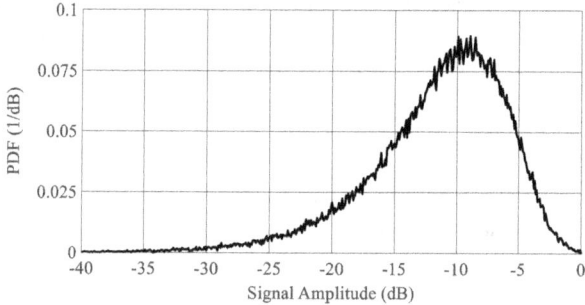

Fig. 2.32: Amplitude probability density function of the OFDM-modulated test signal.

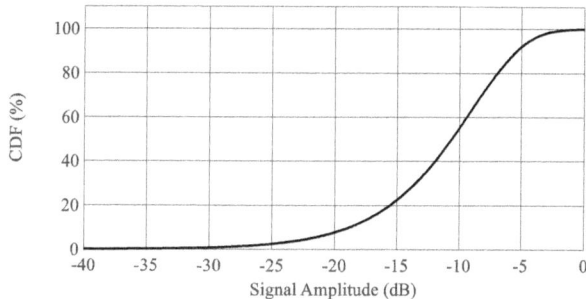

Fig. 2.33: Cumulative amplitude density function of the OFDM-modulated test signal.

The modulator minimum pulse width t_{P_MIN} is calculated based on (15). The modulator control signal is preprocessed to ensure that all pulses have a minimum duration of t_{P_MIN}, and that the supply voltage of the PA is always high enough to avoid overdrive. For a two-level system this removes short pulses of low supply voltage levels and expands short pulses of high supply voltage levels. For a multilevel system the calculation of the optimum sequence becomes more sophisticated, since each manipulated pulse can affect other levels as well. For the generation of the modulator control signal the threshold level (P_{TH}) for each switching level must be defined. In a two-level system there is only a single threshold level which defines whether the lower supply voltage or the higher supply voltage will be switched on. P_{TH} must be chosen according to the maximum allowed output power of the PA for the chosen supply voltage, as derived in Chapter 2.1. P_{TH} represents the power level in dB above the average power of the test signal. The average power level is chosen as reference, since this is intuitively related to the PA which input power will be adjusted to achieve a specified average output power. When class-G modulation with N supply voltage levels is applied, it is possible to split the test signal PDF into N parts. Therefore, for each power supply a PDF for the amplitudes can be derived. The sum of all PDFs equals the original test signal PDF. This is shown in Fig. 2.34 for a two-level class-G system using the test-signal shown in Fig. 2.32 and Fig. 2.33 and a threshold level $P_{TH} = 2$ dB. In (a) the PDF of the amplitudes supplied by the lower voltage supply are shown, in (b) the amplitudes for the higher supply voltage. The PDFs are parametrized with the relative switching frequency f_{REL_G}. For $f_{REL\_G} = 0$ the PDF in (b) equals the test signal PDF, while the probability in (a) is zero for all normalized power levels. This represents the case of fixed supply voltage operation, since the class-G modulator is switched constantly to the high supply voltage. For an infinite f_{REL_G} the PDF is split vertically at the threshold level P_{TH}. This represents the ideal case, where the modulator switches without limitation in minimum pulse length. All values in between show the realistic case, where the modulator switching frequency is limited. With decreasing values, it is seen that more and more power levels below the threshold level are handled at the higher supply voltage, resulting in efficiency degradation. In (a) the PDFs for amplitudes above P_{TH} are all zero since they would cause PA overdrive.

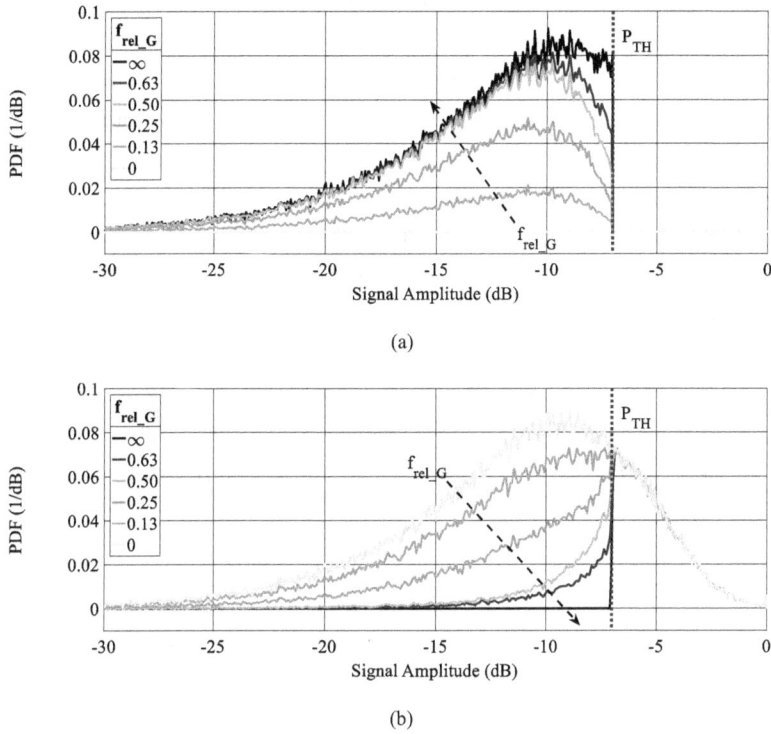

Fig. 2.34: Amplitude probability distribution for a two-level class-G system with different relative modulator switching frequency (f_{REL_G}) constraints for an OFDM modulated signal with 9 dB PAPR. (a) lower supply voltage and (b) higher supply voltage.

The distribution of the signal amplitudes on the different power supplies has a direct impact on the efficiency of the system. In class-G it is targeted to always use the lowest possible supply voltage level. If the switching speed is constrained, then it occurs that a higher supply voltage level will be active for signal power levels below P_{TH}. The distribution of the average power delivered by the power supplies in a two-level system is shown in Fig. 2.35 for the exemplary OFDM test signal. In (a) P_{TH} is fixed at 2 dB, while (b) uses an adaptive P_{TH} that is adjusted with f_{REL_G}. The power is normalized to the power consumed in the static supply voltage case. The calculation is based on a constant DC current multiplied by the supply voltage level for each power supply which according to the characteristics of the DC current shown in Fig. 2.8, is valid for the class-A biased PA:

$$P_{DC} = I_{DC} \cdot \sum_{n=1}^{N} V_{DC}(n) \cdot p_{on}(n) \qquad (17)$$

The amount of supply voltage levels is defined by **N** and each level is weighted by the probability that the power supply is active (**p_on**). For class-AB biasing the DC current becomes a function of the supply voltage and must be calculated for each level separately. As already pointed out by the PDF in Fig. 2.34 (b), for $f_{REL\_G} = 0$ the whole energy is provided by the higher supply level. For $f_{REL\_G} < 0.625$ the almost optimum case is reached. The influence of P_{TH} can be seen by the comparison of (a) and (b) in Fig. 2.35. In (a) P_{TH} is kept constant at 2 dB, which is the optimum value for $f_{REL\_G} > 1$. In (b) P_{TH} is adjusted for each value of f_{REL_G} in a range from 2 to 5.3 dB. Especially for low values, P_{TH} must be increased to achieve optimum efficiency improvement under the constrained f_{REL_G} condition. It can be seen, that for low values of $f_{REL\_G} < 0.5$ the adjustment of P_{TH} is important. One should note here that an adjustment of P_{TH} directly involves a change in the discrete supply voltage level, since P_{TH} sets the required peak power for each supply voltage level. Furthermore, the case (b) shows more constant power consumption for each power supply, dependent on f_{REL_G}.

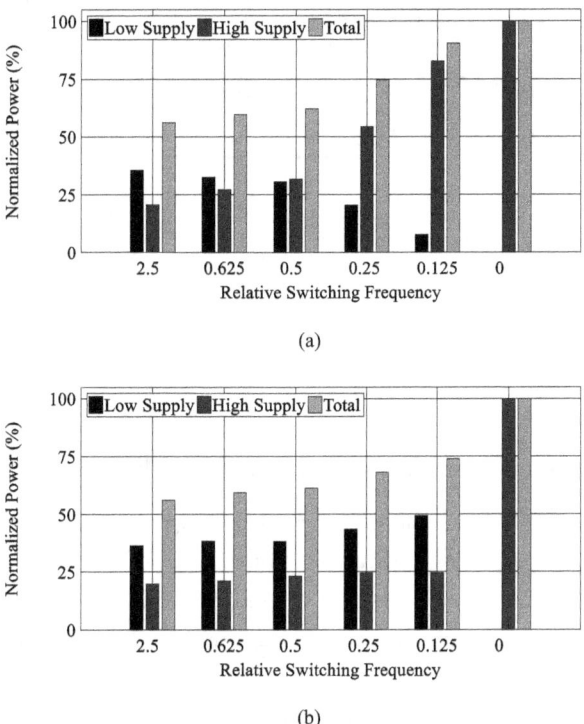

Fig. 2.35: Distribution of the normalized power delivered by the low-voltage and high-voltage supply vs. relative modulator switching frequency for an ideal class-A PA and an OFDM signal. (a) $P_{TH} = 2$ dB, (b) P_{TH} optimized for each f_{REL_G} in a range from 2 dB to 5.3 dB.

The distribution of the power consumption shows, that the maximum switching frequency of the class-G modulator can be lower than the IQ modulation bandwidth of the test signal, while the efficiency improvement is still high. For systems with more than two supply voltage levels the analysis becomes more complex since multiple threshold levels must be defined for optimum efficiency. As shown in Table 1 the use of more than two supply voltage levels allows reducing f_{REL_G} by maintaining constant total power consumption. This constitutes an important advantage for class-G modulation when it comes to extremely broadband modulated systems, where the IQ modulation bandwidth is much higher than the possible supply switching frequency. The simulation results show that, in case of a five-level system, still 50% less dissipated power can be achieved with a maximum switching frequency of only 45% of the IQ modulation bandwidth.

Table 1: Maximum switching frequency requirement as function of the number of supply voltage levels and the associated reduction of dissipated power. The calculations are based on an ideal class-A PA. The OFDM modulated test signal has 9 dB PAPR.

P_{DC_G}/P_{DC}	2-level f_{REL_G}	3-level f_{REL_G}	4-level f_{REL_G}	5-level f_{REL_G}	6-level f_{REL_G}
40%	---	---	---	2.4	1.95
45%	---	---	1.20	1.00	0.95
50%	---	0.95	0.55	0.45	0.45
60%	0.60	0.30	0.25	0.20	0.20
70%	0.25	0.15	0.15	0.15	0.10

---: condition not achievable

2.3 Efficiency enhancement limits of class-G supply modulation

The maximum efficiency enhancement of class-G supply modulation depends on the number of voltage levels used, the maximum switching frequency of the class-G modulator (discussed in Chapter 2.2), and the PA class of operation. For an ideal supply modulator, i.e., a modulator without switching losses and limitations in switching frequency, the best efficiency is achieved when the number of supply voltage levels is going towards infinity. In this case the class-G system converges to a linear envelope tracking system, which is not implementable in practice. Besides that, the higher number of supply voltage levels lowers the modulator efficiency since there are more transistors to be driven and the higher complexity of the modulator increases its power dissipation. At the same time, the efficiency improvement with increasing number of supply voltage levels saturates. Together, this leads to a maximum in efficiency improvement for a certain number of supply voltage levels. This is investigated in the following for different modulation schemes. The analysis considers the amplitude PDF of the test signal, which significantly influences the efficiency improvement, as well as the efficiency of the modulator and the power amplifier. The goal is to analytically find the number of supply voltage levels for a given setup in terms of maximum efficiency. The following analysis uses the supply voltage and power back-off level dependent PA characteristics discussed in Chapter 2.1 for an idealized PA.

The efficiency improvement as function of the number of supply voltage levels is analyzed for three different signal types: An OFDM modulated signal with 9 dB PAPR, a WCDMA signal with 6 dB PAPR and a two-tone signal with 3 dB PAPR. Fig. 2.36 shows the signal amplitude (a) PDFs and (b) CDFs. The PDF and CDF functions differ significantly for the analyzed test signals and the comparison of the CDFs reveals that the amplitudes are distributed on a wider range for the OFDM signal than for the WCDMA or the two-tone signal. This effect is cause by the higher PAPR of the OFDM signal. For class-G modulation this has a significant impact on the efficiency improvement that can be achieved.

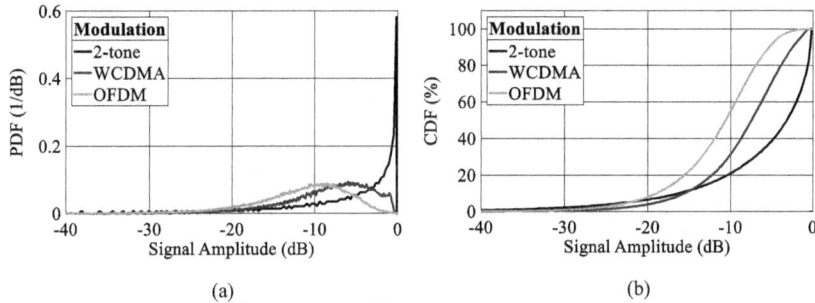

Fig. 2.36: Amplitude (a) probability distribution function and (b) cumulative distribution function of a two-tone signal with 3 dB PAPR, a WCDMA signal with 6 dB PAPR and an OFDM signal with 9 dB PAPR.

The efficiency improvement in class-G systems is based on the reduction of the dissipated power. With the assumption of a constant DC current consumed by the RF PA, e.g., a class-A PA, the power delivered by the power supply is calculated based on (17). The reduction of the power consumption is plotted in Fig. 2.37 for the three test signals, with supply switching threshold levels optimized for efficiency.

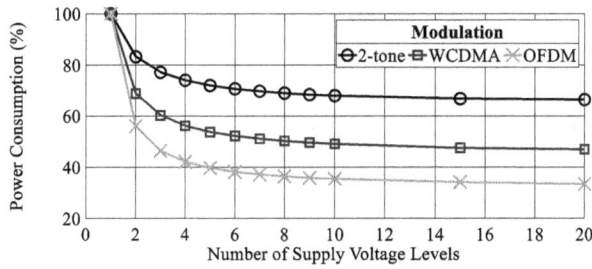

Fig. 2.37: Reduction of power consumption of an ideal class-A PA as a function of the number of discrete supply voltage levels for signals with different PAPR.

It shows that for the signals with higher PAPR the possible power consumption reduction is higher. Besides that, the relative improvements with more supply voltage levels are higher compared to signals with low PAPR. This effect is caused by the fact, that for the case without supply modulation the PA efficiency is higher for the signal with lower PAPR, since the required power back-off level is lower. Translating the results from Fig. 2.37 into the drain efficiency η_D clarifies the situation, which is shown in Fig. 2.38 for the ideal class-A (a) and class-B (b) PA. For the class-A PA the efficiency improvement measured in percentage-points is not related to the PAPR of the signal, since the maximum efficiency achieved with supply modulation decreases linearly with the average output power (Fig. 2.7). For the class-B biased PA it can be stated, that signals with higher PAPR allow more efficiency improvement than signals with lower PAPR, since the efficiency without supply modulation is lower for a signal with higher PAPR and the maximum efficiency achieved with supply modulation is independent of the average output power. More precisely, the higher PAPR requires an increased number of supply voltage levels. This can be verified by the comparison of the efficiency improvement shown in Fig. 2.38.

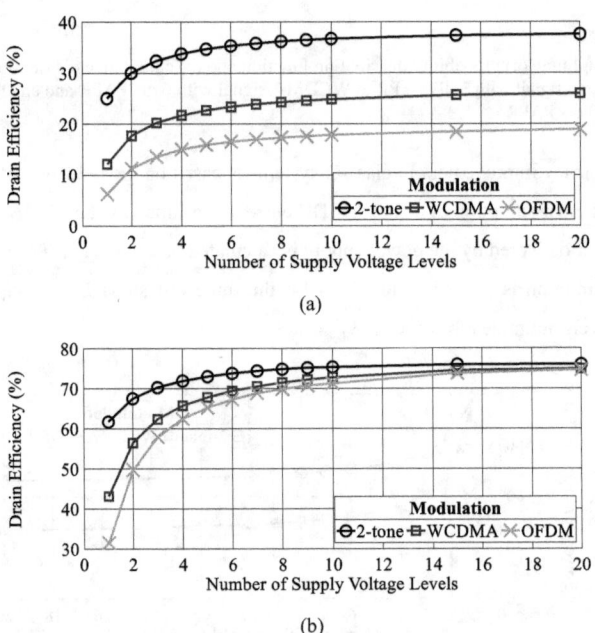

Fig. 2.38: Efficiency improvement as function of the amount of supply voltage levels for different modulation formats with different PAPR, for (a) a class-A biased and (b) a class-B biased PA.

In Fig. 2.38 the modulator is assumed to be 100% efficient. In practice, the efficiency of a class-G modulator is very high but not ideal. Depending on the topology, static and dynamic losses reduce the efficiency of a modulator [28]. The losses can be separated into losses in the transistor gate driver circuit, which in [28] are independent of the switched supply voltages and load impedances, i.e., the output power of the modulator, and the switching stage losses which scale with output power. For low output power levels, it is important to minimize the losses in the gate driver circuit. Chapter 4.1.1 gives more information on the gate drivers and different implementations. For the following analysis the modulator losses are set to depend on the switching frequency and the number of supply voltage levels. The number of supply voltage levels influences the static driver losses in the modulator. The switching stage losses are counted only once and are calculated based on the average switching frequency of the class-G modulator control signal. The following analysis is only a simplified description of the losses that occur in a real system. It would become significantly more complex when taking into account all factors, e.g., the changing load impedance and the impact on the switching stage efficiency. Besides the reduction in complexity the results are more general and less hardware-specific. The dataset used for extraction of the modulator losses is shown in Fig. 2.39 for (a) the gate driver losses and (b) the switching stage losses which are based on measurements of a class-G supply modulator. The gate driver losses show an almost linear increase with the switching frequency. Linearly approximated they consist of a static dissipated power of $(N-1) \cdot 170$ mW, i.e., 170 mW for each transistor switch in the modulator, and dynamic losses of 2.3 mW/MHz. The switching stage efficiency is shown for different load impedances. It also decreases almost linearly with the switching frequency. For the linear approximation a static efficiency of 97.5 % and a decrease of -8.5 percentage-points per 100 MHz are assumed.

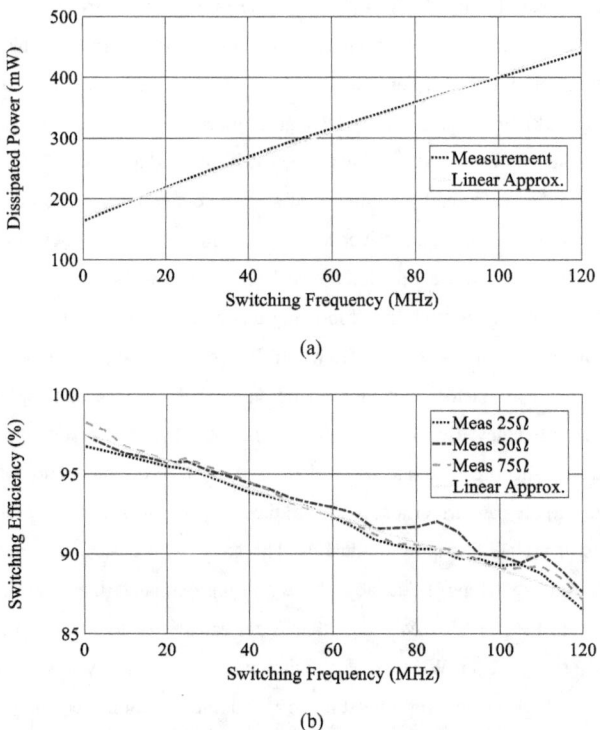

Fig. 2.39: Power dissipation in (a) the gate driver and (b) efficiency of the switching stage as function of the supply switching frequency for a two-level class-G modulator [28]. The supply voltage is switched with 50% duty-cycle between 20 V and 40 V and different load impedances.

The modulation bandwidth does not influence the efficiency of the system in the analysis with an ideal supply modulator. With the realistic modulator model, the modulation bandwidth must be considered as well, since the average supply switching frequency increases linear with the modulation bandwidth. The IQ modulation bandwidth of the three test signals is set to 5 MHz. The efficiency enhancement including modulator losses is shown in Fig. 2.40 for an ideal PA with a peak output power of 60 W. The average output power depends on the signal PAPR, e.g., 30 W for the 2-tone, 15 W for the WCDMA and 7.5 W for the OFDM signal. Comparing the results for the simulations with and without modulator losses one finds that (a) the class-A PA does not show efficiency improvement for $N > 10$ and (b) that for the class-B PA the efficiency is decreased significantly for $N > 7$. This is mainly caused by the static losses of the class-G modulator, which become more dominant if the overall power consumption of the PA is low. As a result, the drain efficiency decreases for the high PAPR OFDM signal already for configurations with more than seven supply voltage levels, peaking at only 60%. In this case the class-G modulator should be optimized to consume the least possible quiescent power.

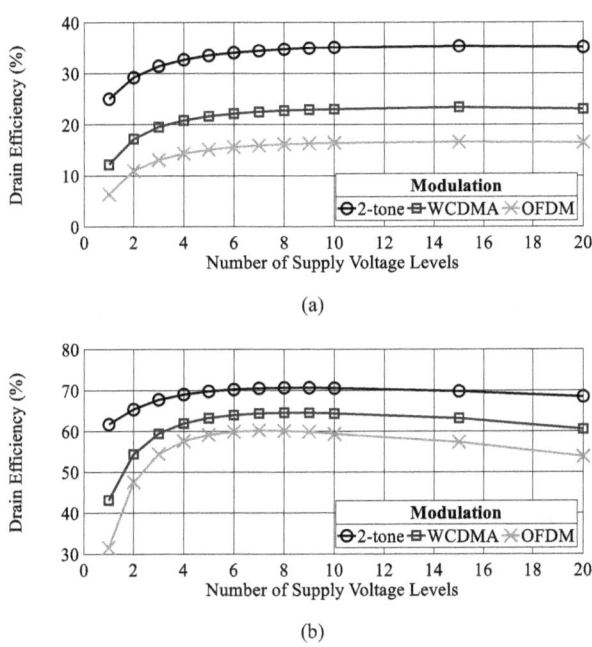

Fig. 2.40: Efficiency improvement as function of the amount of supply voltage levels for different modulation formats with different PAPR including modulator losses, for (a) a class-A biased and (b) a class-B biased PA with 60 W peak output power.

2.4 Power amplifier linearity under class-G supply modulation

For linear amplification, the PA must provide a constant magnitude and phase of the complex valued gain/transmission coefficient (G) over the full modulation band and output power range. Any variation results in a distorted PA output signal. In the previous chapter it is observed that the magnitude of the gain depends on the PA class and power back-off, as shown in Fig. 2.10. Based on the theory of linear and reduced conduction angle PAs, the supply voltage modulation does not further influence the gain of the PA. This emphasizes the choice of the PA operating point in class class-A, class-B or deep class-AB only.

2 Theory of Class-G Supply Modulation

In a practical PA implementation based on GaN technology, it is observed that $\underline{G}$ diverges from the ideal theory and shows a supply voltage dependency for its magnitude and phase [20], [21]. Furthermore, if the PA is driven into saturation, the magnitude of the transducer power gain compresses and a phase shift between input and output signal is observed. With class-G supply modulation, as with any other supply modulation, both mechanisms introduce distortions to the output signal and will be addressed in the following.

2.4.1 Baseband signal distortions caused by gain and phase variations

For the evaluation of the linearity $\underline{x}_{BB}(t)$ is defined as the IQ-modulated baseband signal, consisting of the in-phase component $x_I(t)$ and the quadrature component $x_Q(t)$:

$$\underline{x}_{BB}(t) = x_I(t) + j \cdot x_Q(t) \tag{18}$$

The measured baseband signal at the PA output is defined as $\underline{y}_{BB}(t)$. Like the input signal it consists of an in-phase and a quadrature component, $y_I(t)$ and $y_Q(t)$, respectively. For a system without memory, the signal $\underline{y}_{BB}(t)$ is derived according to (19) with $\underline{G}(|\underline{x}_{BB}(t)|)$ as nonlinear function.

$$\begin{aligned}\underline{y}_{BB}(t) &= y_I(t) + j \cdot y_Q(t) \\ &= \underline{G}(|\underline{x}_{BB}(t)|) \cdot \underline{x}_{BB}(t), \quad \underline{G}: \mathbb{R} \to \mathbb{C}, \quad x \mapsto y\end{aligned} \tag{19}$$

The magnitude of $\underline{G}$ affects the in-phase and quadrature component equally, but the phase variation causes IQ impairments which can be interpreted as an input power dependent rotation of the constellation diagram.

2.4.2 Impact of class-G supply modulation on the transducer gain

For the simplified quasistatic model used in the previous chapter, the phase variation of the gain factor is not addressed, since it depends on reactive components which are not modelled. Dynamic measurements show that also the phase is changing with the supply voltage and output power. Therefore, it has a significant contribution to the overall nonlinear behavior of the PA. In Fig. 2.41 $\underline{G}$ extracted from modulated measurements of a GaN-based PA under dynamic class-G supply modulated operation is shown vs. normalized output power for three different bias points. Memory effects have been removed by averaging. For the magnitude and phase of $\underline{G}$ a sharp discontinuity is observed at a level of -6 dB output power, where the threshold level for switching of the supply voltage between the lower level of 24 V and the higher level of 40 V is located.

Furthermore, it is observed in Fig. 2.41 (a) that the magnitude of $\underline{G}$ diverges from the theoretically derived value in the power back-off region. The behavior is equivalent to a reduction of the conduction angle, i.e., the magnitude of the gain factor for the class-B bias point decreases with reduced output power and matches the expected gain for class-C. Thereby, the magnitude of $\underline{G}$ for the lower supply voltage level is reduced in general. The quasi-static simulations (Chapter 2.1.3), where the I-V knee region is considered, show only a minor reduction of the gain with the supply voltage in the range from 5 V to 40 V. Therefore, the static I-V knee cannot be the root cause of this phenomenon. An explanation for the observed reduced conduction angle is found by taking the existence of trapping effects in the GaN-HEMT into account. The trapping effects are discussed later in Chapter 3.2.

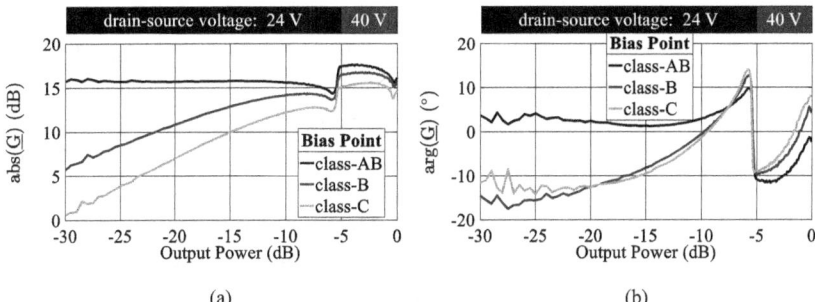

Fig. 2.41: (a) gain and (b) phase variation as function of the output power for different bias points and two-level class-G supply modulation.

For further investigation of the conduction angle the bias point is swept for the lower supply voltage level and output powers below -6 dB as shown in Fig. 2.42. A dynamic gate-bias modulation is applied synchronously with the class-G supply modulation. The gate-bias at the supply voltage level of 40 V is kept constant at the class-B condition. With increased gate-source bias voltage it is seen that the flatness of $\underline{G}$ is improved for magnitude and phase in the power back-off region below -6 dB. The estimated behavior for the magnitude of $\underline{G}$ of a class-B biased PA can be achieved by increasing the gate-bias voltage for the 24 V region. The discontinuity of $\underline{G}$ at the switching threshold is reduced for the magnitude, but the phase increases with the gate-source bias voltage from 20° to 30°.

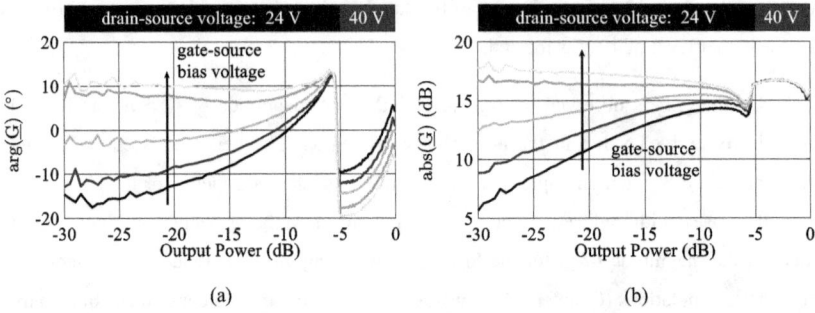

Fig. 2.42: (a) gain and (b) phase variation as a function of output power for different bias points and two-level class-G supply modulation with additional gate-bias modulation for the lower supply voltage level.

2.4.3 Quantification of nonlinear distortions in class-G supply modulated PAs

In the previous subsection it was shown that the magnitude and phase of the transducer power gain varies with the supply voltage levels and the output power. The impact of the magnitude and phase variations at the discontinuity and at different supply voltage levels will be investigated in the following for systems with fixed gate-bias level and for the case of synchronous gate-bias modulation.

For the quantification of the linearity degradation, the adjacent channel leakage ratio (ACLR) (20), error vector magnitude (EVM) (21) and normalized mean-square error (NMSE) (22) are calculated. The ACLR is used to quantify the out-of-band emission in relation to the power inside the modulated band. Here $\underline{X}$ denotes the Fourier transform of the signal. The ACLR can be calculated for the upper and lower adjacent band. If only one value is given for the ACLR, the adjacent band with the worse ACLR is chosen. The EVM is calculated in the frequency domain, too, and defines the average error vector of all complex-valued modulated OFDM subcarriers. Therefore, the EVM only quantifies errors inside the modulated band. It should not be confused with a second possible definition of the EVM which is calculated in the time domain and not used in this work. For this purpose, the NMSE is used, which is the time domain error of two complex valued signals. It quantifies in- and out-of-band distortions.

$$\text{ACLR}(\underline{X}) = 10 \cdot \log_{10}\left(\frac{\sum_{f=\text{inband}}|\underline{X}(f)|^2}{\sum_{f=\text{adjacent band}}|\underline{X}(f)|^2}\right) \quad (20)$$

2 Theory of Class-G Supply Modulation

$$\text{EVM}(\underline{X}, \underline{Y}) = \sqrt{\frac{\sum_f |X(f) - Y(f)|^2}{\sum_f |X(f)|^2}} \qquad (21)$$

$$\text{NMSE}(\underline{x}, \underline{y}) = \frac{\sum_n |x(n) - y(n)|}{\sum_n |x(n)|} \qquad (22)$$

For the quantification of the linearity degradation, a simple model for the observed distortions is defined. Based on the characteristics shown in Fig. 2.41 for a class-AB condition, the supply voltage switching mainly introduces a gain discontinuity (Δgain) and a phase discontinuity (Δphase). For the following analysis, the impact of Δgain and Δphase as function of the supply switching threshold level is investigated for a system with two discrete supply voltages and a single discontinuity. The influence of each parameter is visualized in Fig. 2.43 (a) for Δgain discontinuity and (b) for Δphase with reference to the switching threshold level.

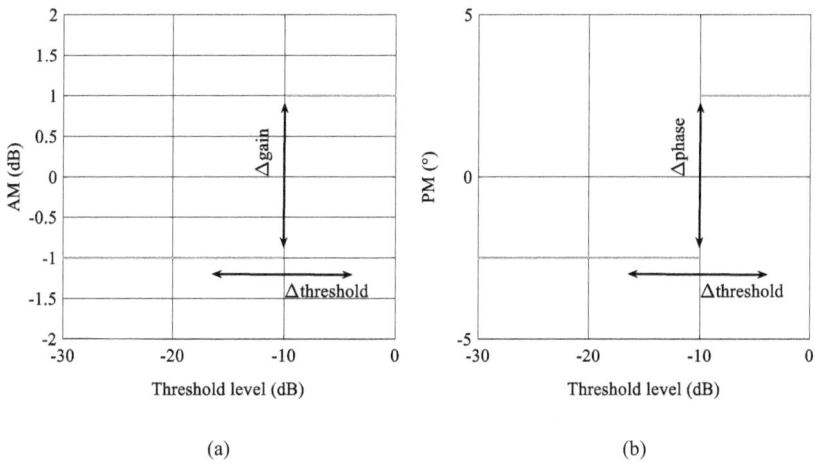

Fig. 2.43: Simplified distortion model for class-G supply modulated operation. (a) Δgain and (b) Δphase.

The trajectories of the distortions caused by Δgain and Δphase are visualized in Fig. 2.44 for a single complex valued sample of the signal. For Δgain it is shown that I and Q are equally affected by a linear amplitude scaling. For Δphase the impact on I and Q is different and depends on the trigonometric functions.

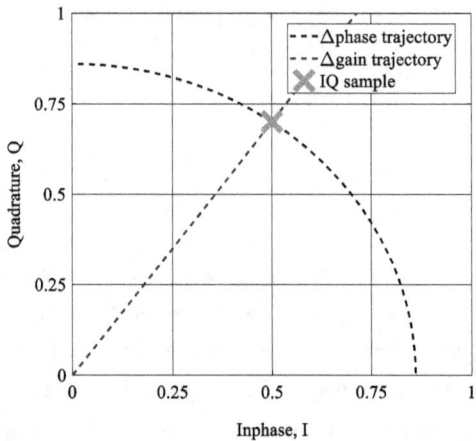

Fig. 2.44: Trajectory of Δgain and Δphase distortions.

The distortion model describes a signal distortion in the time domain. For the NMSE it is therefore possible to calculate the worst case NMSE value in dependence of Δgain and Δphase. Therefore, the time domain distorted signal is defined as:

$$\text{err}(x, \Delta\text{gain}) = \underline{x} \cdot \left[0.5 \cdot \left(10^{\left(\frac{\Delta\text{gain}}{20}\right)} - 1\right)\right] \\ = |\underline{x} - \underline{y}| \quad (23)$$

$$\text{err}(x, \Delta\text{phase}) = \sin\left(\frac{\Delta\text{phase}}{2}\right) \\ = |\underline{x} - \underline{y}| \quad (24)$$

For the definition of (23) and (24) only half the value of Δgain and Δphase is used since the optimum amplitude and phase of the reference signal must be in the middle of the discontinuity for the worst case scenario, where 50% of the signal is below and 50% above the threshold level. The quantification of the worst-case error signal allows the calculation of the NMSE in dependency of Δgain and Δphase. The results are shown in Fig. 2.45 (a) and (b), respectively.

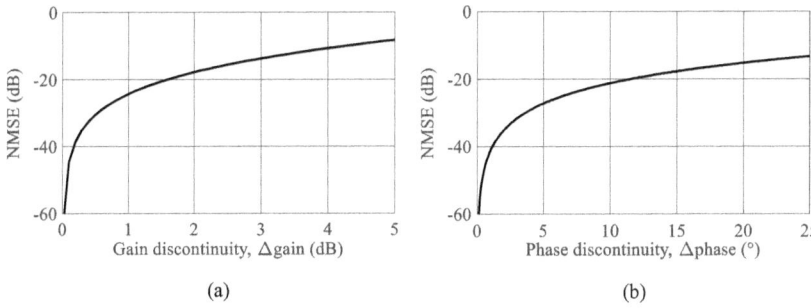

Fig. 2.45 Worst case NMSE degradation vs. (a) Δgain and (b) Δphase.

Further investigation of the impact of nonlinearities, e.g., in the frequency domain and threshold level dependent, requires the specification of a modulated test signal. The signal amplitude PDF, which depends on the modulation format, is important here, since it defines the weight of each amplitude region on the total distortions. The amplitude PDF and CDF of the signal are presented in Fig. 2.32 and Fig. 2.33, respectively. For the evaluation of the impact of Δgain and Δphase on the linearity, simulations for different threshold power levels are conducted.

The impact of the gain discontinuity vs. the switching threshold level is shown in Fig. 2.46 for (a) ACLR, (b) EVM and (c) NMSE. The threshold level has a major impact on the linearity degradation with a peak at ~2.5 dB. The dependency on the threshold level is due to the amplitude PDF of the signal. It is shown that the linearity degradation increases for larger Δgain. The spectra for selected threshold levels and a fixed Δgain of 1 dB is shown in Fig. 2.46 (b). It is seen, that the threshold level affects the total power of the distortion as well as the frequency response. One observes a stronger variation of the in-band distortions than of the out-of-band emission.

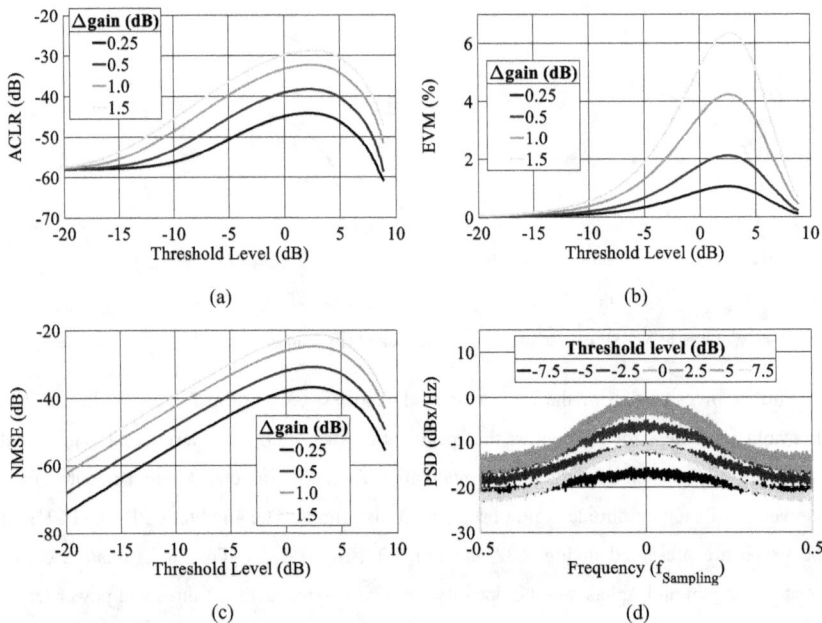

Fig. 2.46: Simulation results for various Δgain values vs. the switching threshold level for an OFDM modulated signal (flat phase, Δphase = 0)). (a) ACLR, (b) EVM, (c) NMSE and (d) PSD of the error signal for different threshold levels and Δgain = 1 dB.

The results for various levels of Δphase vs. the threshold level are shown in Fig. 2.47 (a) to (c) for ACLR, EVM and NMSE. The impact of the switching threshold level on the PSD is plotted in Fig. 2.47 (d) for a fixed Δphase of 2.5°. The comparison of the linearity degradations caused by Δgain and Δphase shows almost similar results.

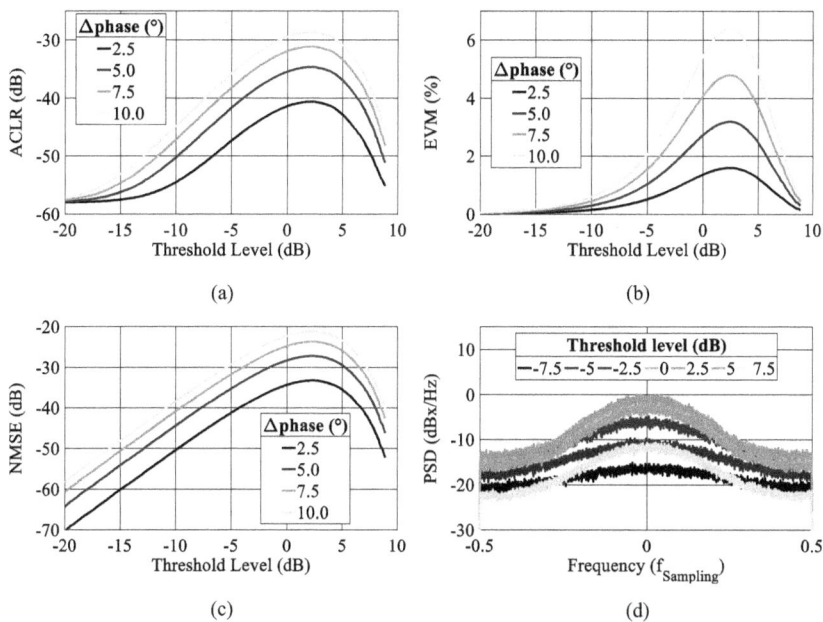

Fig. 2.47: Simulation results for various Δphase and flat gain (Δgain = 0) vs. the switching threshold level for an OFDM modulated signal. (a) ACLR, (b) EVM and (c) NMSE for different Δphase. (d) PSD of the error signal for different threshold levels and Δphase = 2.5 °.

2.5 Conclusions

The analysis of PAs with class-G in the previous sections reveals the flexibility and possibilities of a class-G supply modulated system. Many parameters, e.g. the selection and number of supply voltage levels, the PA biasing and the required maximum modulator switching speed must be chosen properly. The statistics of the amplified signal play a key role in this process. The analysis of the RF PA showed that PA classes with a deep class-AB bias point are preferred for supply modulation. Also, it revealed that class-G supply modulation is particularly suited for broadband systems since the required switching frequency of the modulator can be lower than the IQ modulation bandwidth. The simulations demonstrated that already a two-level system allows a significant efficiency improvement. For more than two levels the improvement increases but saturates very quickly. When modulator losses are considered, the number of supply voltage levels should not exceed six levels in most cases because a higher number of levels yields only marginal improvement.

3 RF Power Amplifiers for Supply Modulation

A PA for supply modulation is operated with a variable supply voltage. Contrary to a static supply voltage PA, it is not optimal to design the matching networks for a single supply voltage. The available supply voltage range and the PDF of the signal amplitudes play a key role in the optimization process. Furthermore, it must be ensured that the PA is stable under all supply voltage conditions. A widespread technique in the design of supply modulated systems is the continuous wave (CW) load-pull characterization at various supply voltages of the transistor to be deployed. With the signal statistics considered, the theoretical optimum reflection coefficients can be calculated and used to design the input- and output matching networks. In practice, the design process becomes more complex, since the GaN-HEMT characteristics depend also on the thermal conditions and memory effects play a role [11]. This chapter concentrates on the GaN-HEMT devices used and the PA design process.

3.1 The RF power GaN-HEMT

For the design of RF PAs devices based on several semiconductor technologies are available. The choice of technology depends on the required output power, frequency, and cost. To date, GaN-HEMT devices offer the highest output power and best efficiency in the frequency range from a few GHz up to at least ~30 GHz. A drawback is the higher cost compared to mainstream silicon technology. In line with the majority of research in this field, GaN-HEMTs were used in this work. The devices were designed and fabricated at the Ferdinand Braun Institute (FBH). Since the RF power transistor in a PA has a key role in the entire system, the following subsection concentrates on that specific part. Especially for GaN-based PAs, effects like a slow compression of the gain under continuous wave (CW) operation [12] and drain/gate-lag effects [13], [14] are observed, which are caused by charge trapping in the device and generally referred to as memory effects.

3.1.1 The Gallium-Nitride III-V semiconductor properties

Gallium-Nitride (GaN) is a III-V compound semiconductor material with high bandgap that offers a high electric breakdown field strength. The key material parameters for GaN and selected other semiconductors are listed in Table 2. Although the electron mobility of bulk GaN is lower compared to III-V semiconductors like GaAs, it offers several advantages: The mobility is increased if a two-dimensional electron gas (2DEG) is formed and, most importantly, the high saturation velocity combined with the high electrical breakdown allows the operation with high supply voltages and high currents or reduction of device size with reductions of parasitics for operation at maintained voltage. Another positive effect of the high bandgap energy is the possibility to operate GaN devices at high temperatures, where, e.g., silicon-based (Si) devices could not be operated. Furthermore, the thermal conductivity is at the same level as Si and significantly higher than for gallium arsenide (GaAs). However, the thermal conditions are mainly determined by the substrate the GaN epitaxial layer is grown on. Hence, if silicon carbide (SiC) substrates are used as in this work, excellent heatsinking performance is achieved.

Table 2: Material properties of selected semiconductors [15].

		Si	GaAs	GaN
Bandgap energy	[eV]	1.1	1.42	3.39
Electron mobility	[cm^2/Vs]	1350	8500	1200, bulk 2000, 2DEG *
Saturation velocity	[cm/s]	10^7	10^7	$2.5 \cdot 10^7$
El. Breakdown field	[MV/cm]	0.3	0.4	3.3
Thermal conductivity	[W/(cm·K)]	1.5	0.43	1.3
* 1200-1700 cm/s according to [16]				

3.1.2 Epitaxial and device structure of a GaN-HEMT

The classical GaN transistor is of the HEMT type. In a HEMT, a heterojunction with conduction band discontinuity is used to create a thin layer of carriers along this junction, the so-called 2DEG, where the electrons have higher mobility than in bulk material. Since the 2DEG is formed in an un-doped layer, high carrier densities can be achieved without a tradeoff in mobility. Contrary to other HEMT types, a GaN-HEMT can be fabricated without the need of additional dopants in the layer next to the 2DEG [16]. By growing a layer of Al$_x$G$_{1-x}$aN on a GaN buffer the lattice mismatch of both semiconductors causes mechanical stress, which results in piezoelectric polarization (p_{PE}). In combination with the spontaneous polarization (p_{SP}) of GaN and Al$_x$Ga$_{1-x}$N, which increases with X, this induces the accumulation of charges at the interface surface as compensation for the polarization charges. This is equivalent to doping and creates the sheet carrier density in the 2DEG. The epitaxial structure used for the GaN-HEMT fabrication is shown in Fig. 3.1 (a). To create a controllable device, ohmic contacts for source and drain and a Schottky barrier contact for the gate have to be realized. The resulting GaN-HEMT structure is shown in Fig. 3.1 (b).

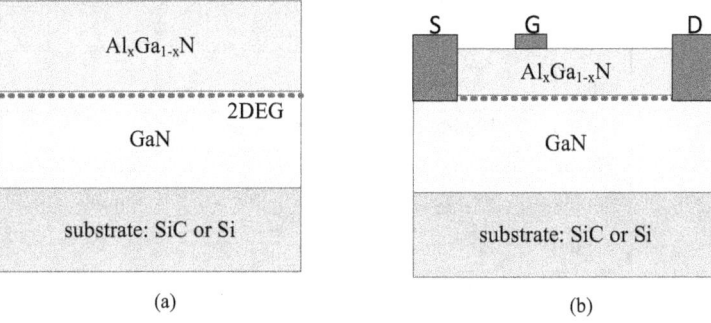

Fig. 3.1: (a) Epitaxial structure of a wafer used for fabrication of GaN-HEMTs and GaN-diodes and (b) a GaN-HEMT device with external contacts. Dimensions are not on scale.

3.1.3 Electrical characteristics of the FBH GaN-HEMTs

GaN-HEMT devices based on the epitaxy shown in the previous subsection are normally-on transistors. The transistor is controlled via a Schottky barrier gate, which controls the charge density in the 2DEG channel. For negative gate-source bias voltages the carrier density in the 2DEG is reduced down to pinch-off. For enhanced breakdown voltages the distance between gate and drain is larger than the gate-source distance, but principally it is possible to operate the device in reverse direction. This has the effect, that under normal conditions reverse blocking capabilities are not given, since for negative drain-source voltages the drain acts as source and may open the channel. In case of a class-AB PA this is not critical, but for the class-G modulator topologies implemented, reverse blocking capabilities are required (see Chapter 4.1).

The GaN-HEMTs designed and fabricated at the FBH are available in different sizes. The gate length of the technology used is 500 nm, with a gate finger length of 250 µm or 400 µm. Multiple transistor cells are combined in powerbars. The characteristics and parameters of a selected set of transistors are shown in Table 3. The thermal resistance between the transistor channel and the package is given by R_{TH}.

3 RF Power Amplifiers for Supply Modulation

Table 3: Overview of the FBH GaN-HEMTs used for the RF PA and class-G modulator design.

Code	Finger length	Total gate width	R_{TH}	I_{DS_MAX}	V_{DS_MAX}
5x8x250	250 μm	10 mm	2.0 - 2.4	6.0 A	200 V*
5x8x400	400 μm	16 mm	1.9 - 2.3	9.6 A	200 V*
11x8x250	250 μm	22 mm		13.2 A	200 V
11x8x400	400 μm	35.2 mm		21.1 A	200 V

*: Different gate-drain distances available, which influences V_{DS_MAX}.

For the computer-aided design of RF PAs a large-signal transistor model is used. The model used to characterize the FBH GaN-HEMTs is based on the Chalmers model [19]. Using this model, it is also possible to model the impact of self-heating due to dissipated power in the transistor. As shown in Fig. 3.2 (a) and (b), self-heating in the transistor has a significant impact on its DC characteristics and thus R_{TH} is important, e.g. for the maximum power dissipation. For the DC characteristics shown it is impossible to operate the transistor in a class-A bias point with a quiescent current of 3 A at V_{DS} = 40 V, since the dissipated power would exceed the safe operating area (SOA) where the average dissipated power is below 60 W. For single supply PAs this would be a significant drawback and limit the possible output power, but not for a class-G supply modulated system, since the dissipated power is significantly reduced which expands the SOA.

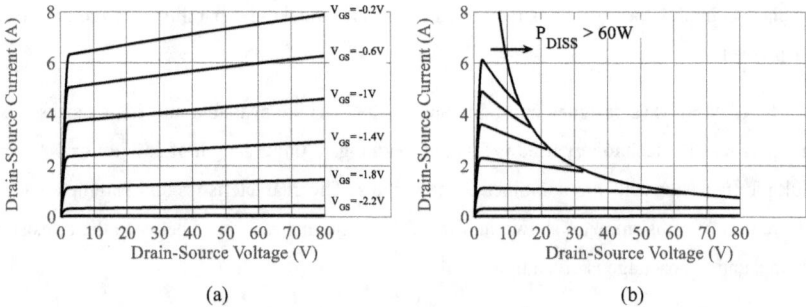

Fig. 3.2: DC-characteristics of the 5x8x400 GaN-HEMT, (a) without and (b) with self-heating effects.

However, there is an important difference between CW and non-CW operation. In a PA handling a broadband modulated signal, the duration of the high-power signal peaks is short and thus the temperature does not instantaneously follow the dissipated power due to thermal capacitances, which buffer the temperature [17]. Therefore, the average dissipated power can be used to calculate the temperature increase for rapidly changing signals. Thus, the transistor output characteristics as shown in Fig. 3.2 (b) are not valid for a dynamic operation. The impact on the saturated I_{DS} as function of the temperature is shown in Fig. 3.3. With increasing temperature, the saturation current is reduced. For the knee I-V region it is observed that the transistor on-resistance (R_{ON}) increases with temperature while the knee voltage is reduced due to the lower maximum I_{DS}. It must be noted that the results shown do not incorporate any memory effects which occur in dynamic operation.

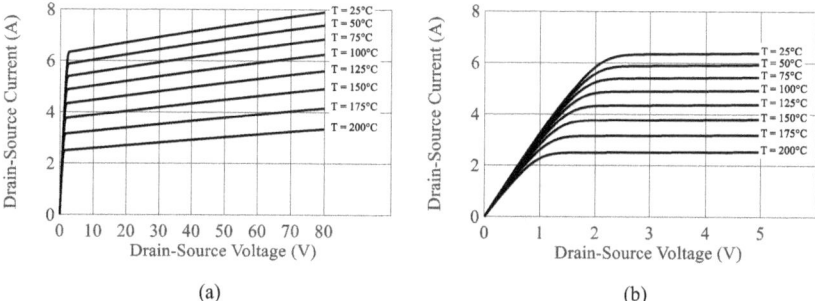

Fig. 3.3: I_{DS} degradation of the 5x8x400 GaN-HEMT as function of the transistor temperature without self-heating. Full characteristics (a) and knee I-V region (b).

The main purpose of a PA is to amplify a signal. Hence, a key parameter of a PA is the power gain, which depends on the transconductance (g_m) of the transistor:

$$g_m = \frac{\Delta I_D}{\Delta V_{gs}} \quad (25)$$

As can be seen from Fig. 3.2, thermal self-heating has a strong impact on the drain current, which causes a degradation of g_m. This is illustrated in Fig. 3.4, where g_m is extracted from simulations of the transfer characteristics using the Chalmers model (a) without and (b) with self-heating enabled. In Fig. 3.4 (b) the temperature increase depends on the drain-current and therefore increases with the gate-source voltage. If the PA is operated with RF excitation, the temperature increase is based on the average dissipated power and, therefore, independent of the gate-source voltage. The impact of a constant temperature change on g_m is shown in Fig. 3.5 (a) for absolute values and (b) for the relative change Δg_m. It can be seen, that an increased temperature causes a significantly reduced g_m with an almost linear relationship in the temperature range under investigation.

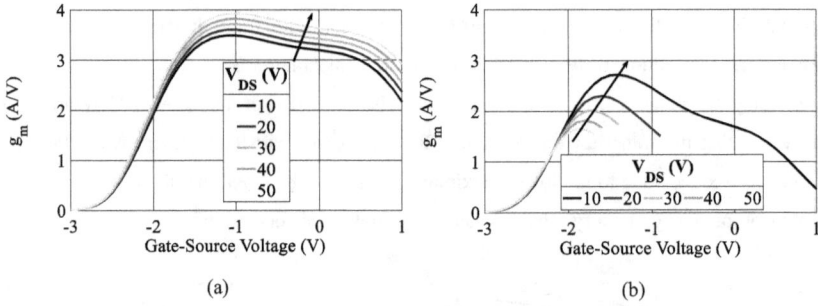

Fig. 3.4: Transconductance vs. gate-source voltage (a) without and (b) with self-heating for different V_{DS}.

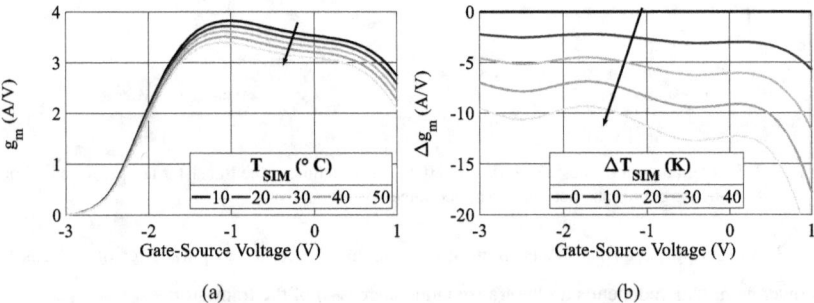

Fig. 3.5: Transconductance (a) and g_m deviation (b) for selected simulation temperatures for different gate-source voltages and $V_{DS} = 40$ V.

To investigate the impact of thermal self-heating on the matching, load-pull simulations at 2.7 GHz were conducted and are shown in Fig. 3.6 for (a) PAE contours and (b) P_{OUT} contours. The temperature between transistor package and channel is calculated based on the dissipated power and a thermal resistance of 2.2 K/W. The ambient temperature is set to 25 C. For low dissipated power levels where the temperature increase is below 100°C, no influence on the optimum load impedance is visible for PAE and P_{OUT} optimization. For higher temperatures, the PAE and P_{OUT} contours are more compressed for the simulations using the GaN-HEMT model with self-heating. An important effect of the increased temperature which is not visible in Fig. 3.6 is the influence on the transducer power gain and the saturated output power. For ΔTEMP of 80°C the gain is reduced by 1.1 dB and the saturated output power by 0.8 dB, giving $P_{SAT}(\Delta TEMP=80°C) = 47.5$ dBm.

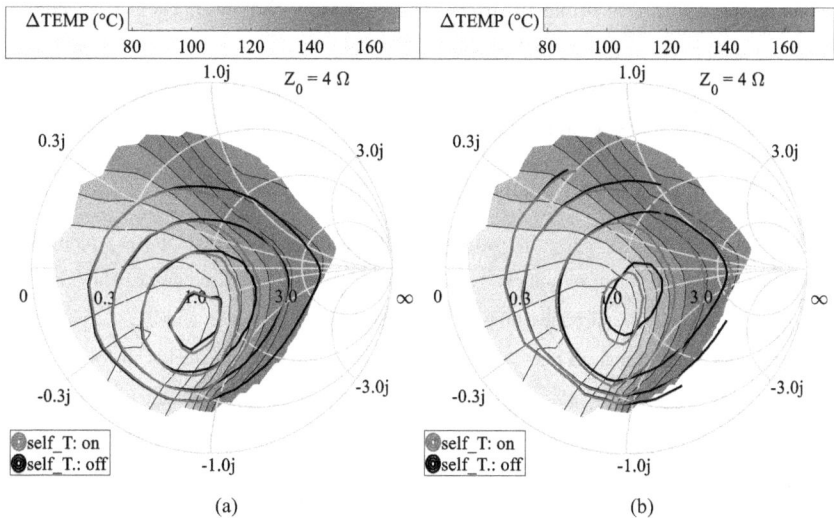

Fig. 3.6: Load-pull simulation contours at 2.7 GHz with and without self-heating effects (self_T) for a class-AB PA, optimized for (a) PAE and (b) P_{OUT}. P_{AVS} adjusted for same maximum P_{OUT}. PAE step size 10%-points and P_{OUT} step size 2 dB. $V_{DS} = 40$ V and the quiescent $I_{DS} = 700$ mA.

The simulations show that the thermal effects are of high importance for the design of efficient PAs. In supply modulated systems the conditions are more relaxed due to the reduced dissipated power. Most significant is the influence on the maximum output power and gain. It shows, as expected, that higher peak output power levels can be achieved if the efficiency is increased by supply modulation.

3.2 Impact of charge-trapping in GaN-HEMTs on RF performance

GaN-based high-power devices have developed rapidly in the past. Although the material quality has improved, the performance of the devices still suffers from charge trapping effects. During the course of this work, it was found that the effects caused by charge trapping are of high importance in the design of supply modulated RF PAs since they result in a dispersion between static and dynamic characteristics of current/voltage and gain. The problem for supply modulated PAs is that the optimum bias and matching condition depends on the supply voltage range and signal statistics. Therefore, the PA is usually characterized over a wide supply voltage and power back-off range to estimate the efficiency under dynamic operation, as will be discussed in Chapter 3.3.2. The common way to acquire these measurements is to use a load-pull setup to become independent of a transistor model. It was found during this work, that the dispersion between the CW and dynamic supply modulated measurements is not negligible and requires careful considerations. Two dominant effects are visible: gate-lag and drain-lag. The quantification can be done by dynamic I-V measurements, where the quiescent bias point is modified.

3.2.1 Dynamic I-V measurements

For the quantification of the charge trapping, dynamic I-V measurements are widely used. In this set-up, the transistor output characteristics are measured in pulsed mode. The transistor is biased for a long time (around 500 µs) in a quiescent bias condition and the I-V points are measured only within a short pulse around 200 ns, so that only fast effects can follow while slow mechanisms such as device temperature and most of the traps cannot and stay at the quiescent level.

The measurement results of a single 8x250 µm GaN-HEMT cell are shown in Fig. 3.7 for (a) gate-lag and (b) drain-lag. For the identification of the gate-lag, the quiescent V_{DS} is kept at 0 V, while for the gate-source bias two different quiescent voltages of -7 V and 0 V are selected. For the drain-lag quantification two quiescent points for V_{DS} at 0 V and 50 V are selected. Based on this separation, it is shown that the gate-lag influences the slope of the transistor transfer curve, i.e., g_m while, the drain-lag causes a shift of the pinch-off voltage (ΔV_{GS}) which influences the bias point.

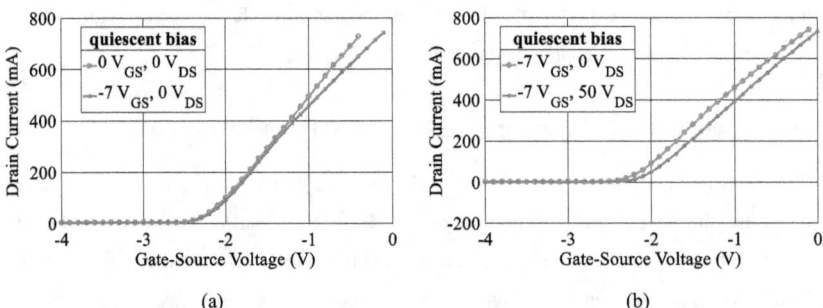

Fig. 3.7: Dynamic I-V measurements for (a) gate-lag quantification and (b) drain-lag quantification. The measurements are performed at V_{DS} = 40 V.

The V_{DS} dependency of gate-lag and drain-lag is important if the PA is operated with supply modulation. The effects observed in Fig. 3.7 for a variation of the quiescent gate-source and the quiescent V_{DS} are quantified as a variation of g_m (Δg_m) and the gate-source pinch-off voltage offset (ΔV_{GS}). The comparison of the dynamic I-V measurement is shown in

Fig. 3.8 for (a) Δg_m and (b) ΔV_{GS}, referenced to the trap quiescent condition of $V_{GS} = 0$ V and $V_{DS} = 0$ V. The coefficients are extracted for fixed V_{DS} over a V_{GS} range from -2.5 to 1 V. Therefore, the extracted Δg_m is an average value over the gate-source voltage range. For Δg_m it is observed, that the quiescent V_{GS} adds a constant Δg_m difference of 11% over the full range of V_{DS}. Independently of the quiescent bias voltages, almost no dependence on V_{DS} is visible. The gate-source voltage offset shows a different behavior. Here a behavior independently of the quiescent V_{GS} is observed, while the quiescent V_{DS} introduces a constant pinch-off voltage shift ΔV_{GS}. For quiescent $V_{DS} >= 30$ V an almost linear dependency of ΔV_{GS} is observed

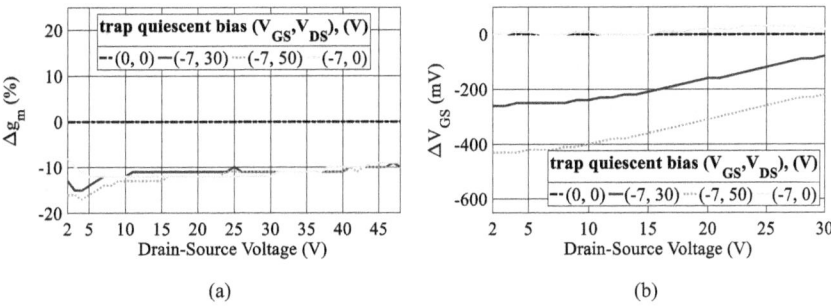

Fig. 3.8: Comparison of dynamic I-V measurements for gate-lag and drain-lag quantification. (a) transconductance variation (Δg_m) and (b) gate-source pinch-off voltage shift (ΔV_{GS}), referenced to dynamic measurements vs. V_{DS}.

The comparison of static and dynamic measurements is shown in Fig. 3.9 (a) for Δg_m and (b) for ΔV_{GS}. Thereby the influence of thermal self-heating is visible. The average dissipated power is significantly higher for the static measurements, which causes the observed V_{DS} dependency of Δg_m, since thermal heating has a significant impact on the slope of the I-V characteristics of GaN-Schottky diodes [29], which is the controlling element in a GaN-HEMT.

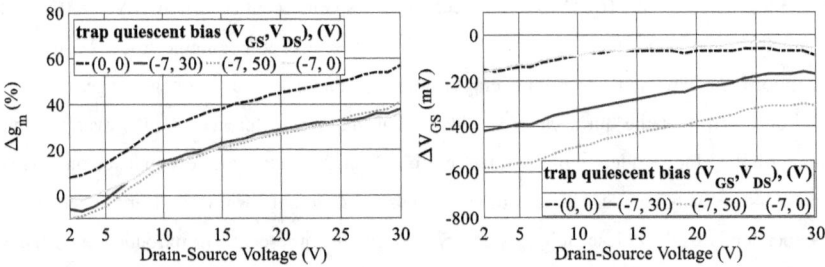

Fig. 3.9: Comparison of static and dynamic I-V measurements for gate-lag and drain-lag quantification. (a) transconductance (Δg_m) variation and (b) gate-source pinch-off voltage shift (ΔV_{GS}), referenced to static measurements vs. V_{DS}.

The previous measurement showed the average of Δg_m over the full gate-source voltage range. To investigate the impact of the gate-source voltage on Δg_m, the coefficients are evaluated for fixed V_{GS} over a V_{DS} range from 3 to 48 V. The results for Δg_m are shown in Fig. 3.10. The compensation for ΔV_{GS} is applied according to Fig. 3.8 (b). For V_{GS} above -2 V Δg_m is almost flat. In the region below -2 V a strong influence for high trap quiescent V_{DS} is visible, although it does not scale with the absolute level of the trap quiescent V_{DS}.

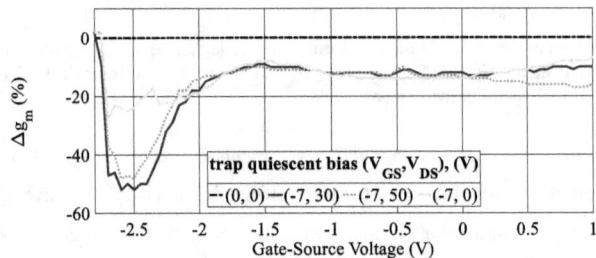

Fig. 3.10: Comparison of dynamic I-V measurements for gate-lag and drain-lag quantification. Transconductance variation (Δg_m) referenced to dynamic measurements vs. gate-source voltage.

Recent work set the focus on the drain-lag effect since it is seen to be more dominant in state-of-the-art GaN-technology [30]. Due to the dependency on V_{DS}, drain-lag effects also become more dominant if supply modulation is applied. Large deviations from CW measurements are observed for reduced supply voltages. Then, trapped charges located close to the gate act as a negatively biased virtual gate which influences the bias point [31]. Much attention has been paid to these phenomena. It was found that the charge trapping and de-trapping effects have different time constants. The charge de-trapping can take up to several seconds, depending on the temperature and bias point, while the charge trapping almost happens instantly within picoseconds and is mainly set by the instantaneous peak level of the drain voltage [32], [33], [34]. Since the trapped charges shift the gate-source voltage dependent g_m characteristics towards higher gate-source voltages the quiescent bias current will be reduced, and the PA changes its class of operation towards lower conduction angles.

3.2.2 Slow compressive gain and its relation to gate-lag

For GaN-based PAs a slow compression of the transducer power gain (G_T) is observed in CW measurements, as shown in Fig. 3.11 (a). Thereby it is seen, that G_T slowly decreases over a wide output power range, starting already 15 dB below the saturated output power. An explanation for this effect is found in the observed effects of charge trapping [12]. It can also be derived from the influence of gate-lag and thermal heating on g_m. Only if the bias point is close to class-B, the drain-lag induced shift of the gate-source pinch-off voltage can cause an additional significant gain-compression due to a bias shift to class-C.

For a PA operated with a CW signal, the root mean square (RMS) of the RF gate-source and drain-source voltage is constant and therefore the trapped charges are in a fixed state. In a slow CW power-sweep, the trapped charges have enough time to settle. The influence of the charge trapping will increase with the output power. The gate-lag reduces g_m while the drain-lag reduces the conduction angle. This causes the PA to operate more efficiently but with a reduced gain compared to an ideal device without charge trapping effects. If the PA is operated with a modulated signal, the RMS value of the RF drain-source voltage will vary according to the envelope of the modulated signal. At high voltages the trapping states are charged, and the trap-state is maintained during lower voltages due to their large de-trapping time constants. As a result, the charge trapping becomes independent of the instantaneous voltage and no soft compression is observed. This can be verified by the measurements shown in Fig. 3.11 (b) for a 16 MHz bandwidth OFDM modulated signal with 9 dB PAPR. A slightly increased G_T at saturated output power is seen for the modulated signal. This could be caused by a more relaxed thermal condition due to a lower average dissipated power under operation with a modulated signal with high PAPR. At back-off the G_T is lower for the modulated because of the reduced conduction angle in combination with the reduction in g_m.

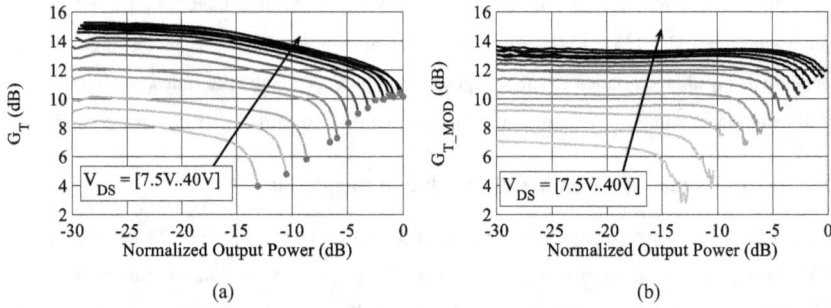

Fig. 3.11: Power sweep of the transducer power gain (G_T) of a GaN-HEMT based RF power amplifier operating at 2.7 GHz with V_{DS} from 7.5 to 40 V. Continuous wave (a) and 16 MHz bandwidth, 9 dB PAPR (b) excitation.

3.2.3 Drain current degradation in relation to the drain-lag

The major impact observed for drain-lag is related to the drain current and therefore has a significant impact on the efficiency under modulated operation. The shift of the gate-source pinch-off voltage affects the bias-point and the drain current consumption at power back-off, which is investigated in [35]. There, the drain-lag is modelled as a virtual gate-source bias voltage (v_{TRAPP}) that is induced by the trapped charges and dependent on the maximum drain-source voltage (V_{DS_MAX}). During operation of the PA with a wideband modulated signal, the V_{DS_MAX} will depend on the peak output power of the signal and v_{TRAPP} becomes a steady value. Hence, the instantaneous effective gate-source bias voltage (v_{GS_EFF}) is set to be:

$$v_{GS\_EFF}(t) = v_{GS}(t) + v_{TRAPP}(V_{DS\_MAX}) \qquad (26)$$

The impact off v_{TRAPP} on the drain current is shown in Fig. 3.12 for three different class-AB DC quiescent bias voltages, measured with a 1.8 GHz CW signal. For low output powers the conduction angle is 360°, therefore a constant drain current is expected according to the theory. But the measured current shows a decrease with increased output power, marked as ΔI_D. At power levels around 34 dBm the conduction angle starts to decrease due to the large v_{GS} excitation and the drain current starts to increase.

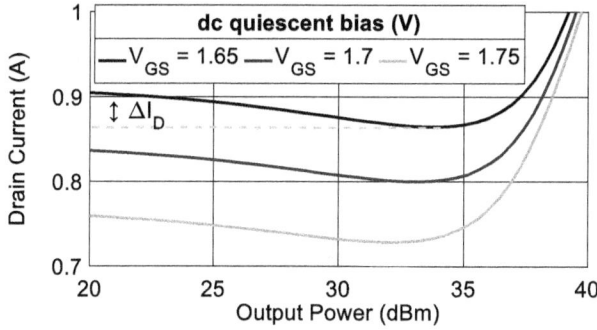

Fig. 3.12: Drain current measurements in a CW power sweep with different dc quiescent gate-source bias voltages and $V_{DS} = 40$ V at 1.8 GHz.

According to the hypothesis that the increased V_{DS} impacts the drain-lag and is causing a shift of the threshold gate-source voltage, a relation between ΔI_D and the drain-source voltage difference ΔV_{DS} can be extracted:

$$\Delta I_D = \gamma \cdot \Delta V_{DS} \qquad (27)$$

For the dataset shown in Fig. 3.12 the coefficient γ is 6.1 mA/V for the dc gate-source bias voltages shown. V_{DS} is calculated based on the output power, since a constant load impedance is applied to the transistor. This allows calculating the required shift in gate-source threshold voltage which equals v_{TRAPP}. The output power dependent V_{DS} and v_{TRAPP} is shown in Fig. 3.13. At maximum output power v_{TRAPP} exceeds 200 mV, which corresponds to a significant shift of the gate-source pinch-off voltage. The quiescent current is reduced by 33%.

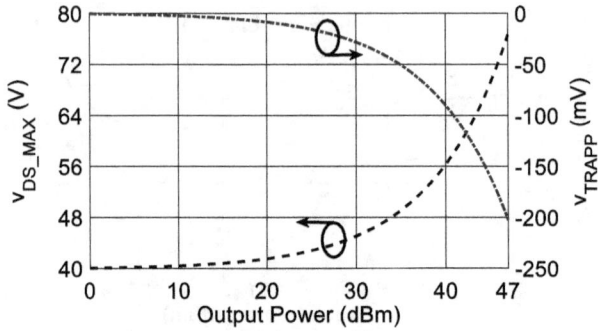

Fig. 3.13: Peak drain-source voltage (V_{DS_MAX}) and trapping voltage (v_{TRAPP}) as function of the output power at V_{DS} = 40 V at 1.8 GHz.

For verification of the hypothesis, the PA is operated with modulated signals with different PAPR. This allows a variation of the peak output power at a constant average output power. The test signal is an eight-tone signal with 4 MHz tone spacing and a constant tone-power. The PAPR is variable in the range from 1.2 to 9 dB and set by adjustment of the phase. The extracted LF drain current for measurements with different peak output power levels is shown in Fig. 3.14. Each color corresponds to a peak output power level. The current is measured in the LF drain bias path with a prototype of a galvanically isolated broadband current sensor developed at the FBH. The measurements show that the peak output power has a strong impact on the dynamic minimum/quiescent drain current, whereas no impact from the average output power is visible. For the average current a slight decrease with increasing peak output power is visible, which is caused by the v_{TRAPP}-induced reduction of the conduction angle. As result, the drain current consumption under modulated operation is lower than calculated based on the test signal amplitude PDF in combination with the CW power sweep measurements. With this result, the modulated measurements prove that the introduction of a peak output power dependent voltage v_{TRAPP} describes the observed current degradation for a wideband modulated signal. The impact of v_{TRAPP} on the output power dependent drain current is shown in Fig. 3.15. It shows that the drain current is mainly influenced in the low-power region, where the conduction angle is almost 360°.

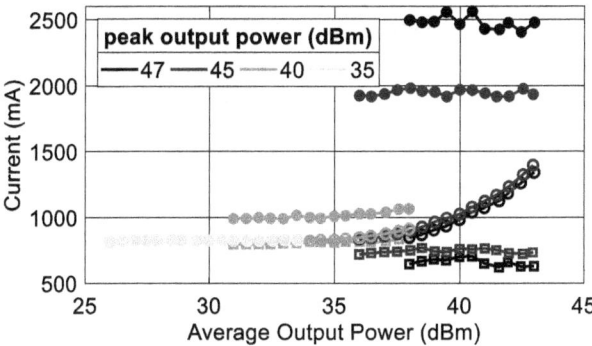

Fig. 3.14: LF drain current measurement as a function of average output power for modulated signals with different PAPR levels. Dynamic peak value (filled dots), average value (empty dots) and minimum/quiescent value (empty squares).

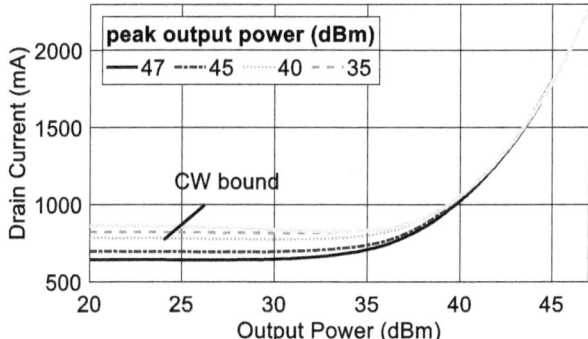

Fig. 3.15: Influence of v_{TRAPP} on the drain current under dynamic operation for different peak power levels (fixed v_{TRAPP}) based on CW measurements.

Finally, the verification is done by calculation of the average drain current consumption under modulated operation with and without the existence of v_{TRAPP} and comparison to the average current measured by the power supplies. The results are shown in Fig. 3.16 as error between measured and calculated current. It clearly shows that the modelling of v_{TRAPP} significantly improves the accuracy of the CW measurement based current calculation to a maximum error of 2.5%, while the calculations without v_{TRAPP} show strong deviations of more than 20% for a combination of high peak output power and high PAPR.

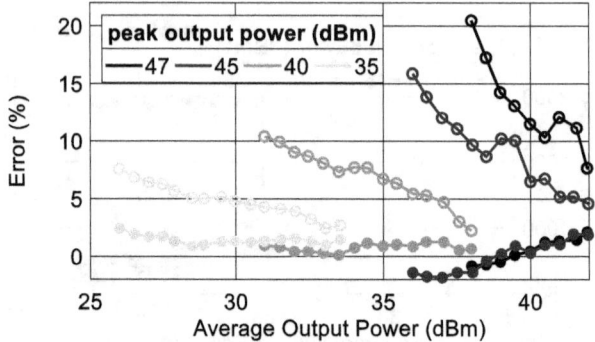

Fig. 3.16: Error of the CW measurement based average drain current for modulated signals when varying the PAPR for two modeling approaches with fixed gate-source bias voltage (empty dots) and with trapping offset voltage (filled dots).

3.2.4 Conclusions

The impact of the observed gate-lag and drain-lag on the efficiency and linearity of the PA depends on the bandwidth of the envelope of the modulated RF signal. For narrowband signals, the charge de-/trapping can follow the envelope and massive distortions will occur since the gain will show the slow compressive behavior, as seen in the CW measurements. With a broadband modulated signal, the de-trapping is too slow to follow the voltage of the envelope signal and better linearity than predicted based on the CW evaluation is achieved.

For the design of class-G supply modulated PAs the observed behavior is challenging, since simulations based on CW simulations or load-pull measurements at fixed supply voltage levels are not valid under modulated operation with varying V_{DS} [11]. For compensation of the drain-lag effects the modelling of a second virtual gate-source voltage (v_{TRAPP}) can be used. For compensation of G_T a further modelling approach is required, otherwise a special treatment to put the traps in a defined state as proposed in [34] might be a valuable solution to increase the accuracy.

3.3 Design considerations for supply modulation

The basic requirement for a supply modulated PA is the stable operation in a defined supply voltage range. It is also important that the operating band is covered for all supply voltages. This is complicated by the V_{DS} dependency of the optimum source- and load impedance for a GaN-HEMT. Therefore, in a system without concurrent dynamic load modulation, the matching networks must be designed with higher bandwidth than usually required, to ensure that the modulation band is covered for all supply voltage levels. Another important aspect is the efficiency as function of the supply voltage. Depending on the amplitude PDF of the modulated signal combined with the available supply voltage levels, the probability that a specific supply voltage level is used can be calculated. With this knowledge, it is possible to design a PA optimized for, e.g., maximum average efficiency.

3.3.1 Supply voltage dependent output impedance matching

For optimum operation the supply voltage dependency of the optimum source- and load impedance must be considered regarding the RF bandwidth and the PAE. The RF bandwidth is dependent on the requirements of the targeted communication standard and must be covered at all possible supply voltage levels. The influence of the supply voltage on the PAE and P_{OUT} contours for a deep class-AB biased 5x8x400 GaN-HEMT is shown in Fig. 3.17. For (a) and (b) the simulation frequency is set to 2.65 GHz and for (c) and (d) to 1.84 GHz. Both frequencies are chosen to investigate the performance of E-UTRA downlink communication bands (E-UTRA band 3 and band 7), which are used for the targeted wireless communication application. As already shown in the theoretical analysis for a class-AB bias point (Chapter 2.1), the reduction of the supply voltage causes the optimum load impedance to increase. In the simulations at 2.65 GHz for supply voltages higher than 20 V the increase is mostly resistive, but can be different for other RF frequencies as shown for 1.84 GHz. On one hand, this is caused by parasitics introduced by the transistor package causing the simulations to deviate from the theoretical approach where the reference plane is directly at the intrinsic transistor current source. On the other hand, the output capacitance of the GaN-HEMT is changing with the supply voltage [36], [37]. The drift of the load impedance with supply voltage must be considered when the matching networks are designed and an impedance with a good trade-off for all conditions must be selected. This fact highly motivates the use of synchronous load-modulation but exceeds the scope of this work. For optimum results, the signal statistics must be considered to calculate the optimum impedance and the required supply voltage range. This is done in the following subsection.

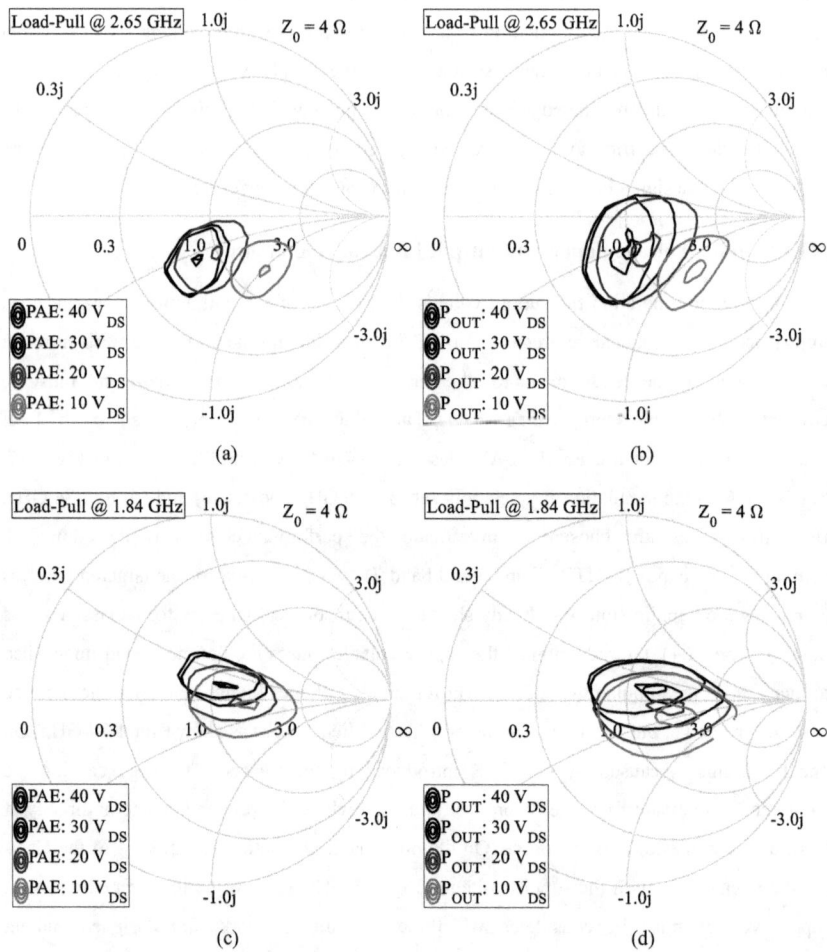

Fig. 3.17: PAE (a), (c) and P_{OUT} (b), (d) contours for load-pull simulations with different V_{DS}. Contour step size for PAE 5 %-points and P_{OUT} -1 dB. 5x8x400 transistor with 700 mA quiescent I_{DS}.

3.3.2 Probability distribution optimized design for class-G supply modulation

For the PAE optimization of a class-G supply modulated PA design, load-pull simulations or measurements are conducted. As shown in the previous subsection, the supply voltage has a significant impact on the performance in terms of PAE and saturated output power, therefore the load-pull data is required for the full supply voltage range of interest. The thus obtained dataset provides information about the efficiency, gain and saturated output power at various supply voltages. This is required since the PA must be optimized not only at its maximum CW output power, but also in the power back-off region. The required power back-off is dependent on the signal statistics of the modulation format used. Most significant is the PAPR of the signal, since it defines how much power back-off is required and therefore the average output power of the PA. The PAPR is derived from the PDF of the signal amplitudes. The PDF of the amplitudes of different bandwidth OFDM modulated baseband signals is shown in Fig. 3.18 (a). All signals are generated with the same sampling rate, but the number of modulated carriers is set to 50, 100, 200 or 400, depending on the bandwidth. This distribution is used in the following to extract the optimum supply voltage levels and switching thresholds for an exemplary PA with PAE back-off characteristic as shown in Fig. 3.18 (b). The PA is based on a 5x8x400 packaged GaN-HEMT, fabricated at the FBH (device introduced in Chapter 3.1.3). The PA is biased with a quiescent I_{DS_Q} of 500 mA (5% of I_{DS_MAX}), which corresponds to a theoretical conduction angle of 186° at $V_{DS} = 40$ V. In this example a fixed input- and output matching is given, since the reference PA was already built. If the designer is still in the design phase, the PAE back-off behavior will depend on the load and source impedances and therefore the following analysis must be conducted for all impedance configurations of interest.

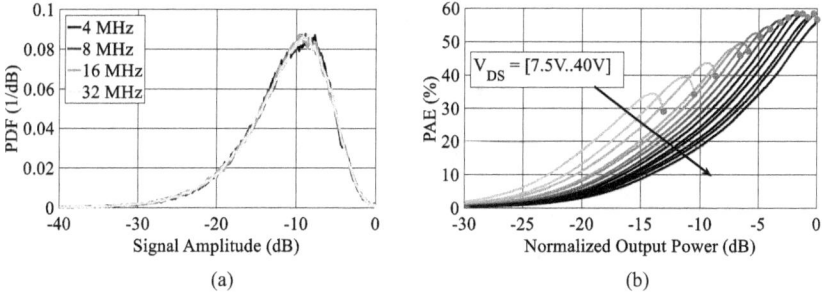

Fig. 3.18: (a) Amplitude PDF for different bandwidth OFDM modulated signals and (b) CW-based PAE measurements of a reference PA with varying supply voltage levels.

With the PDF the contribution of a specific output power back-off range, the overall dissipated power can be calculated as a function of the load impedance and the supply voltage used in the load-pull. In the following analysis it is assumed that the PA is fully linearized which guarantees that the amplitude PDF at the PA output has the identical shape as the signal PDF. Fig. 3.20 shows (a) the PDF of the dissipated DC power and (b) the required RF input power for different supply voltage levels. Since the saturated output power is reduced with the supply voltage, the use of the supply voltages is constrained to the specific saturated output power which is indicated in Fig. 3.20 by the red dots. The segmentation into power back-off ranges is required, since only a limited amount of supply voltages is available with class-G supply modulation. Thus, the possible supply voltages and impedances are limited by the requirement on the saturated output power for the specified output power back-off region as shown in Fig. 3.19. It is seen that the measured saturated output power deviates from the ideal behavior derived in Chapter 2.1.1, where a decay of -20 dB/decade is calculated.

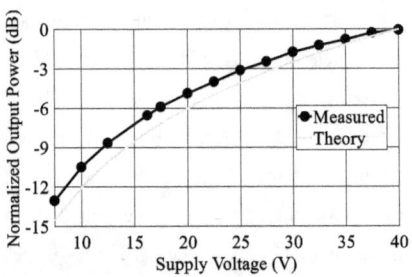

Fig. 3.19: Comparison of measured and theoretical normalized saturated output power as function of the supply voltage.

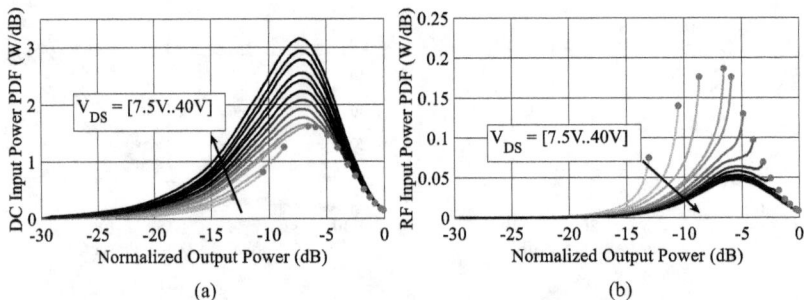

Fig. 3.20: Visualization of the power dissipation PDFs for different supply voltage levels. The red dots indicate the saturated output power which is limiting the use of the specific supply voltage level; (a) dissipated DC input power and (b) RF input power.

For the two-level system, only the lower supply voltage level is variable, since the highest level is fixed to maintain a constant peak output power. The impact of the lower supply voltage level on the power dissipation and therefore the PAE is shown in Fig. 3.21 (a) and (b), respectively. The switching threshold level is derived from the saturated output power as function of the supply voltage level. The higher supply voltage is fixed to 40 V. In the simulations a peak efficiency value for a lower supply voltage level in the range of 17-20 V is derived. The total efficiency improvement is 12%-points and the DC dissipated power is reduced from 32 W to 20 W. This shows that the supply voltage levels are highly important and must be chosen according to the modulation scheme, otherwise the full efficiency improvement will not be achieved. For systems with more than two supply voltage levels the extraction of the optimum values becomes more complex and can be done by, e.g., a recursive optimization process.

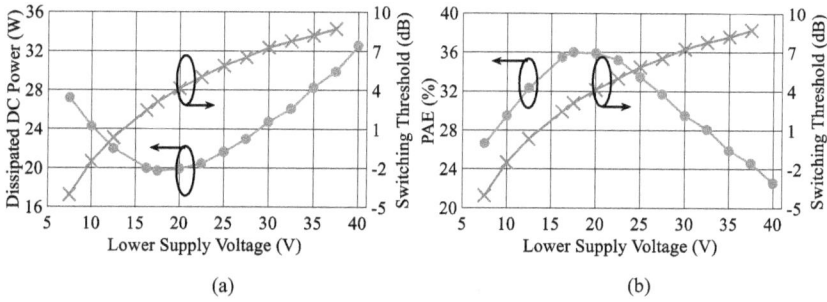

Fig. 3.21: Influence of the lower supply voltage level for two-level class-G supply modulation on (a) dissipated DC power and (b) PAE.

In this work the simulations are based on CW measurements, although it was found during an analysis that the CW-based optimization does not deliver optimum results [11]: A drawback of the CW-based optimization is the expected inaccuracy caused by memory/charge trapping effects which influence the gain and the efficiency due to self-biasing effects [12] (see also Chapter 3.2). Besides that, the thermal heating under CW operation is much higher and will degrade the performance of the transistor as shown in Chapter 3.1.3. Furthermore, the model accuracy of the GaN-HEMT simulation model will limit the quality of the optimized design. This does not influence the theory presented but should be considered during the acquisition of the transistor load-pull simulations/measurements.

3.3.3 Bias circuitry design for class-G operation

The bias circuitry of a PA must implement isolation between the DC/LF and RF path at the in- and output of the PA. Its core element is a diplexer circuit with three ports, which is called bias tee. A schematic of a bias tee is shown in Fig. 3.22 (a). The port p1 is connected to the transistor gate/drain terminal. Port p2 is connected to the gate/drain bias or the gate/supply modulator, depending on the PA. Port p3 is the RF in-/output of the PA. The signal applied at p1 is split into by the diplexer into a DC/LF signal at the low-pass port p2 and a RF signal at the high-pass port p3. The ports p2 and p3 are isolated. A simple implementation of a bias tee is shown in Fig. 3.22 (b). An inductor is used as RF-choke (low-pass) and the DC/LF-block is implemented by a capacitor (high-pass). A schematic of a full PA including the bias tees at the in- and output is shown in Fig. 3.23.

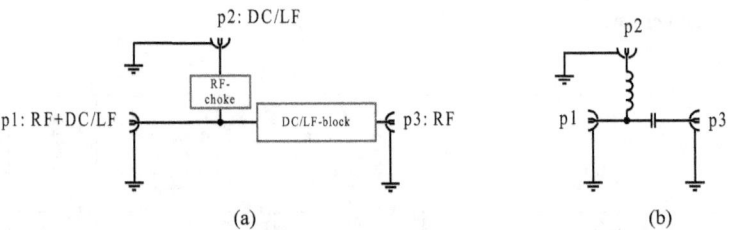

Fig. 3.22: (a) Bias tee diplexer circuit and (b) simple implementation based on an inductor RF-choke and a capacitor DC/LF-block (b).

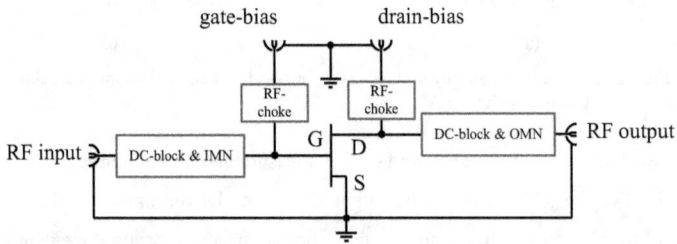

Fig. 3.23: Schematic of a power amplifier with gate- and drain bias tee.

Several implementations of the RF-chokes and DC-blocks are possible, but each implementation has its pros and cons. In most PA designs DC-blocking is implemented by an RF capacitor, operated close to its series resonant frequency to ensure low insertion loss. The most challenging parts are the RF-choke implemented in the drain bias path if the PA is operated with broadband modulated signals and supply modulation: Depending on the amplifier class, variations in the envelope amplitude of the modulated signal cause the drain current to change with input drive level. Especially for reduced conduction angle PAs the drain current will show significant LF modulation. Thereby the bandwidth of the drain current is dependent on the envelope bandwidth. To avoid linearity and performance degradation, the RF choke on the drain side must provide low-pass characteristics with a bandwidth larger or equal to the bandwidth of the modulated drain current. The gate-bias is not that critical, since almost no current is drawn. Therefore, inductances in the bias path do not cause significant voltage drop in the bias path. For systems with high relative bandwidth the design of the RF-choke becomes more sophisticated. It requires a larger low-pass bandwidth for the LF signal and a sharp cut-off frequency to provide the good RF isolation. The impedance seen at the drain terminal, i.e., the load impedance for the low-pass filter, is not constant for most PA classes. The filter must work with varying load impedances and maintain its low-pass characteristics and RF blocking capabilities. Simple filter designs with small number of poles are favorable but depending on the required LF bandwidth and RF isolation difficult to design.

With class-G supply modulation applied, the LF drain bias path becomes even more important than for a system with fixed supply voltage level. For efficient class-G supply modulation the drain bias network must ensure that the slew rate of the modulated supply voltage is not degraded by the low-pass characteristics of the drain bias network. If the modulator slew rate is degraded below the level required by the modulated signal, i.e., the maximum slew rate of the envelope signal, the class-G modulator must be operated to switch the supply voltage earlier to a higher level to avoid the PA to go into compression during the transition. As a result, the efficiency improvement will be reduced. The responses of two different drain bias network implementations are compared in Fig. 3.24 for a 1.8 GHz PA. (a) a $\lambda/4$-wavelength RF choke with 30 Ω characteristic impedance is compared to (b) an 18 μH inductor based RF choke. For the inductor based implementation the short 2.5 ns width supply voltage pulses are degraded for load resistances below 50 Ω. Based on these simulations the $\lambda/4$-wavelength stub is favorable due to its lower impedance in the LF range. One has to pay for this in the RF domain by a reduced isolation bandwidth and, therefore, a possible reduction of the RF bandwidth. For the harmonic load impedances, the $\lambda/4$-wavelength stub might also cause problems, since the even order harmonics are shorted by this topology.

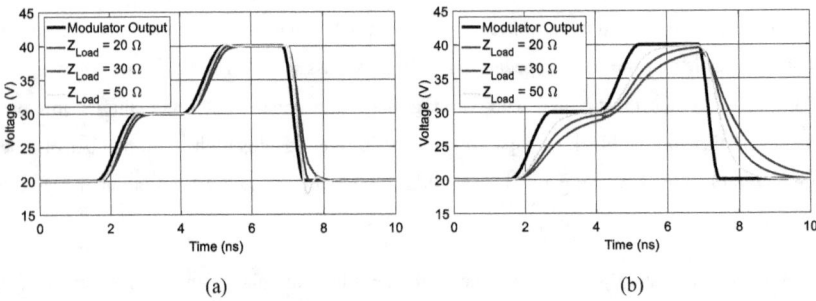

Fig. 3.24: Impact of the drain bias network on the transient response of the supply voltage for resistive loads, based on (a) λ/4-wavelength stub and (b) inductor.

3.3.4 Stability analysis

In a PA, active components that provide power gain, e.g., transistors, are used for amplification of a signal. Each active device with a power gain larger than unity can oscillate if a feedback path when the correct phase is provided. Since amplification is the purpose of a RF PA, the active device feature a high power gain. Therefore, special attention must be paid to the stability analysis to prevent any form of oscillations. In RF designs, small coupling between in- and output can already occur due to parasitics in the transistor resulting in a feedback. Depending on the attenuation and phase of the feedback signal the PA can become instable and start to oscillate. In a PA design this condition should be avoided since it causes unwanted emission, distortion and can lead to destruction of the transistor or other components. Therefore, the designer must stabilize the transistor during the design process to ensure stable operation up to the maximum oscillation frequency of the transistor (f_{MAX}). If the PA is stable for all load- and source impedances in a frequency range from DC to f_{MAX} it is unconditionally stable. If stability is only given for a selected set of impedances the PA is conditionally stable and can only be used in a well-defined impedance environment. For supply modulated PAs, stability must be ensured over the full supply voltage modulation range. Depending on the modulator technology used, the output impedance of the modulator may cause instabilities in the LF range. Especially for closed-loop controlled supply modulators the output impedance for frequencies above the controller cut-off frequency is not well defined. For class-G modulators, the modulator output impedance in the DC to LF range is kept very low, since the supply modulator switches the transistors to defined on- or off-states. This simplifies the stability analysis and reveals class-G supply modulation to be a robust architecture in terms of stability.

3 RF Power Amplifiers for Supply Modulation

The stability analysis used in this work is based on small and large signal S-parameter simulations using a model of the RF GaN-HEMT device. Therefore, the PA is excited with large signal CW signals of different power levels and a harmonic balance solver is used. The large-signal S-parameters are extracted based on the incident and reflected waves. The K-factor (28) can be used to analyze the stability at a single frequency point. For K < 1 the PA is conditionally stable or instable, while for K > 1 the PA is unconditionally stable.

$$K = \frac{1-|S_{11}|^2-|S_{22}|^2+|S_{11} \cdot S_{22}-S_{12} \cdot S_{21}|^2}{2 \cdot |S_{12} \cdot S_{21}|} \quad [38] \quad (28)$$

For the validation of the stability, the K factor is calculated for the full frequency- and supply voltage range. Furthermore, it is suggested to simulate a certain range of bias points, since it is seen for GaN-HEMT devices that the quiescent current might change over time and requires a readjustment of the gate-source bias voltage. Besides the K factor, stability circuits are a valuable tool to determine which in- and output terminations cause possible instabilities. The stability circuits of an exemplary FBH GBT13-01 5x8x400 transistor, biased in class-AB at V_{DS} = 40 V, is shown in Fig. 3.25 for a frequency range from DC to 8 GHz for (a) input stability and (b) output stability.

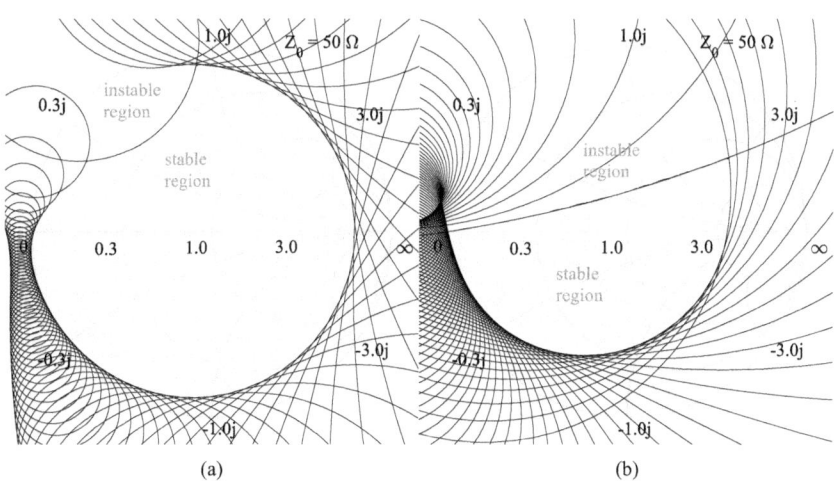

Fig. 3.25: (a) input and (b) output stability circles of a FBH 5x8x400 transistor in class-AB bias at V_{DS} = 40 V for frequencies from DC to 8 GHz.

The device shown in Fig. 3.25 shows conditional stability and, therefore, requires a stabilization network to ensure reliable operation under all load conditions. The stabilization is achieved by introducing losses in the matching network. This reduces the possible input- and output reflection coefficient coverage in the Smith chart. The stabilization is a challenging task since it can reduce the gain and efficiency of the PA depending on the design. It is the goal to introduce the least possible losses in the operation band when stabilizing the transistor to avoid degradation of the power gain. Furthermore, a solution with a small number of components is desired to reduce the risk of malfunctioning due to tolerances/model inaccuracies of the stabilizing components. The stability circuits in Fig. 3.25 show possible instabilities for different in- and output impedances. Stabilizing the input will influence the output stability circuits as well. It is desirable to insert the stability network at the PA input to keep the power dissipation in the stability network as low as possible. Stabilization is achieved by the insertion of series and parallel resistances as shown in Fig. 3.26. Thereby the Smith chart coverage of Γ_{IN} is reduced which enables exclusion of instable regions from the possible reflection coefficients. In case of a parallel stabilization resistor (R_P), the open circuit condition is limited by R_P from the Γ_{IN} reference plane. For a series resistor (R_S), the short circuit condition is limited by R_S. The combination of resistive and reactive components allows frequency selective stabilization of the transistor.

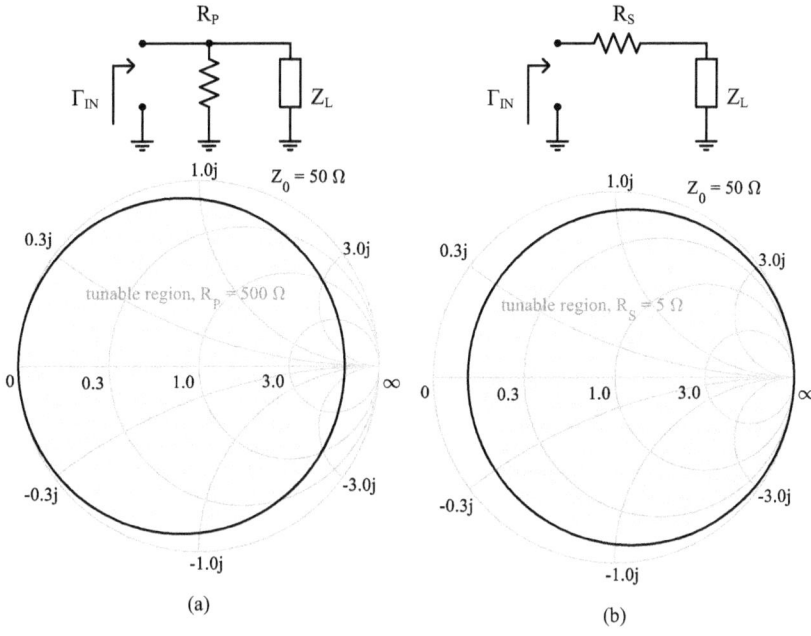

Fig. 3.26: Stabilization circuits and their influence on Γ_{IN} of a tunable load. (a) parallel resistance, (b) series resistance.

4 Class-G Supply Modulators

In a class-G supply modulated PA system, the supply modulator is a multilevel switch that switches the PA supply voltage between two or more discrete levels. The requirements for the class-G modulator are very challenging: Fast switching, low jitter, high efficiency and low output impedance in the full DC to LF range. The LF output impedance is crucial for linearity, since the PA connected to the class-G modulator will provide a low-pass bias network to allow fast supply voltage transitions. Therefore, the class-G modulator must ensure that its output impedance in the LF range is very low to avoid self-modulation effects [7].

The modulators developed in this work are designed to supply PAs in the power range between 50 W and 100 W at a maximum supply voltage of 40 V. For wideband systems with IQ modulation bandwidth beyond 100 MHz, modulators with minimum pulse durations of ~2.0 ns are required to achieve maximum efficiency values. Therefore, the modulator must be operated with maximum switching frequencies of up to 250 MHz. To fulfill these requirements, the modulator designs presented in this chapter are all based on RF power GaN-HEMT technology. For the latest developments GaN Schottky diodes are used since it is seen that Si-based Schottky diodes are limiting the switching frequency due to their large reverse recovery time.

4.1 GaN-HEMT switching stages

A class-G modulator is a multilevel switch which switches the supply voltage of a PA between several already available discrete supply voltages. For this purpose, fast RF GaN-HEMTs have been evaluated [28], [40]. They show superior performance in high frequency switching applications due to their low input capacitance and low switching losses. A drawback of the GaN-technology is that no complementary devices are available (only transistors of n-type). Therefore, the main challenge in the design of a class-G modulator is the implementation of a gate driver for GaN transistors. Two possible switching stage implementations are shown in Fig. 4.1, both suitable for a four-level modulator. The supply voltages (V_1 to V_4) are referenced to GND, which is omitted in the schematic. The output of the switching stage is connected to the drain bias network of the PA. The number of supply voltage levels can be increased by insertion of more intermediate stages, each consisting of a transistor and diode. Both concepts have different advantages. In (a) the transistor drain terminals are connected AC-wise to a common node. This simplifies the design of a multilevel gate driver if p-type transistors are used. Version (b) combines all source terminals to a common node and is therefore preferred if only n-type transistors can be used, e.g., GaN-HEMTs. The transistor gate drivers for configuration (b) must ensure that the gate-source voltage of each switching transistor is constant in the on- or off-state, independently of the source potential. When the modulator is operated, the output voltage of the modulator is switched and therefore the source potentials of the transistors change as well. The gate driver therefore must track the output voltage to keep the transistor in a defined state if all signals are referenced to the GND. Another solution is a floating gate driver, which is galvanically isolated and always referenced to the source potential of the transistor. If an isolated gate driver is used for the implementation of type (a), each transistor requires a separate isolated gate driver. A single isolated gate driver with multiple levels can be implemented for a switching stage of type (b). The modulators designed in this work are based on galvanically isolated gate drivers. The first generation switching stages are based on the topology (a) and replaced by type (b) in the latest designs.

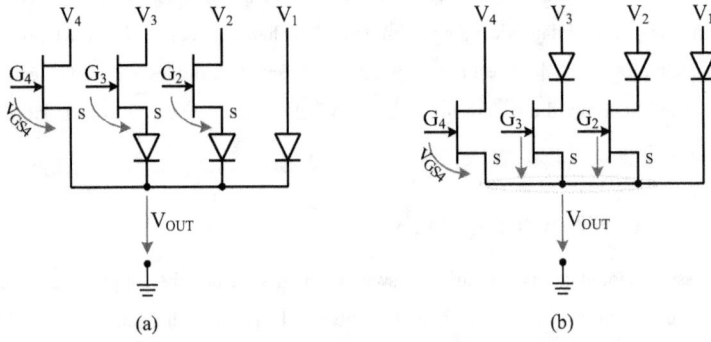

Fig. 4.1: Schematic of a two switching stage implementations for a four-level class-G modulator. Version (a) preferred for p-type and (b) for n-type transistors.

The switching stages shown in 4.1 are designed to use the least required number of active devices. A disadvantage of both topologies is that the output node cannot be discharged actively. The modulator output voltage is always buffered by parasitic capacitances due to the transistors, diodes and gate drivers connected to it. Therefore, the slew rate of the falling edge is dependent on the loading of the output node, i.e., the current consumption of the load. This limits the switching frequency for high impedance loads [28]. A solution for high impedance loads is the implementation of a push-pull stage where a second transistor is used to actively discharge the output node as shown in Fig. 4.2 (a). Thereby it can be ensured, that the modulator output voltage follows the input signal, independently of the load impedance. If GaN-HEMTs are used as switches, the push-pull stage requires a more sophisticated gate driver circuit, since both transistors must be driven with reference to their source potential due to the n-type architecture. For the transistor T_1 the source potential is connected to the modulator output and therefore shows the full output voltage swing, while the transistor T_2 is driven with reference to the fixed level V_1. This is shown for an exemplary waveform in Fig. 4.2 (b), where $V_2 = 40$ V and $V_1 = 20$ V and the gate-source voltage of T_1 and T_2 is driven in the range of -4.5 to 0.5 V. It can be seen, that the amplitude of the gate-source waveforms is different for both transistors, if a ground-referenced driver is used. For a galvanically isolated driver both transistors can be driven with the same amplitude, but two separate drivers with a digital isolator each are required, which cannot be combined as in Fig. 4.1 (b). This might become a problem if phase-jitter is introduced by the digital isolators. It can lower the efficiency, since the timing of the gate signals is not perfectly and a short circuit condition might occur during the transition.

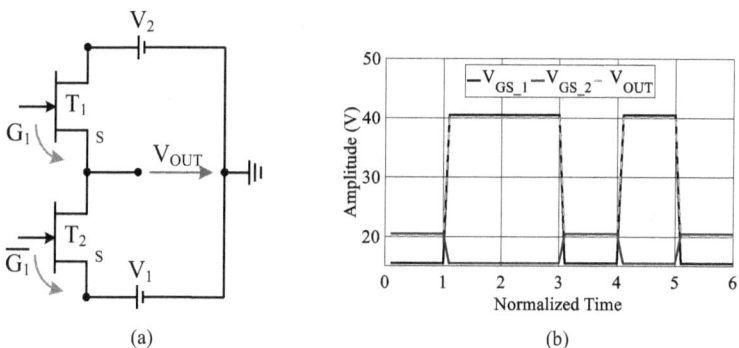

Fig. 4.2: (a) schematic of a two-level push-pull stage and (b) the corresponding gate- and output voltage waveforms.

For the implementations the structure shown in Fig. 4.1 was chosen if the modulator must drive a power amplifier. Modulators with push-pull switching stages were used to evaluate gate bias modulation and for the driving of varactors (not addressed in this work), since in both cases almost no current is consumed by the load.

4.1.1 GaN-based Schottky diodes

The GaN-HEMTs used for switching of the supply voltage cannot block reverse voltage, i.e., negative drain-source voltage. Therefore, modulator switching stages as shown in

Fig. 4.1, require diodes to implement reverse voltage blocking. Another benefit in this architecture is that the lowest supply voltage level has no need for a transistor, which simplifies the design. The diodes must provide an extremely short reverse recovery time, otherwise the minimum pulse length of the class-G supply modulator will be degraded, and a large overshoot of the output voltage may occur. Depending on the supply voltage levels and the supply voltage stage in which a diode is inserted, the breakdown voltage requirement of the diode is different. If no voltage overshoot occurs, the maximum reverse voltage required is defined by the difference between the highest and lowest supply voltage. Since the maximum supply voltage used is in the range of 40 V, many silicon based Schottky diodes are available. For the first modulator prototypes developed in this work, silicon Schottky diodes with reverse recovery time of 3 ns were used [28]. With these diodes the maximum switching frequency was limited to 100 MHz. For the development of faster modulators, a replacement for the slow silicon Schottky diodes was found in GaN-based Schottky diodes. Although they show a significantly higher forward voltage drop, the extremely fast switching capability compensates the DC losses if the modulator is operated at high switching frequencies. Although the diodes were not characterized in detail, modulators with switching frequencies up to 250 MHz have been realized. A comparison of the DC characteristics of a Si Schottky diode (ZLLS500, Diodes Inc.) and a GaN Schottky diode (12 mm diode, FBH) is shown in Fig. 4.3. The Si diode features a significantly lower forward voltage than the GaN diode. For low switching frequencies this is advantageous but with increased switching frequency the dynamic losses dominate and the GaN-diode becomes the first choice.

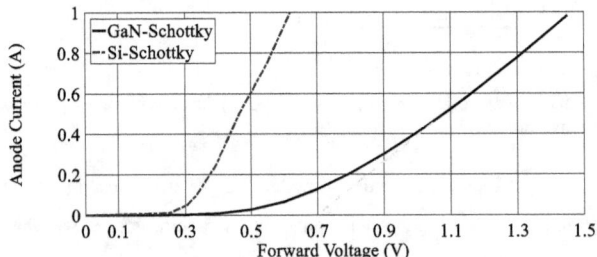

Fig. 4.3: DC characteristics of a ZLLS500 Si and a 12 mm GaN Schottky diode.

4.2 Galvanically isolated gate drivers

The switching stages shown in the previous section are based on GaN-HEMTs designed for RF applications. These transistors have two aspects which must be considered in the design of a gate driver: First, the transistors are "normally on" transistors and require a negative gate-source voltage to be switched of, and second no complementary devices are available, and all transistors are controlled by the gate-source voltage.

The gate drivers designed for the different class-G modulator implementations are all based on a galvanically isolated circuit where the driver floats with the source potential of the transistor. The gate driver is supplied by a galvanically isolated DC/DC converter and a galvanically isolated digital isolator is used to establish the data link between the ground-referenced input and the floating part of the driver. The floating part of the gate driver is designed to use the GaN-HEMT source node as virtual ground reference and therefore operates floating with regard to system ground. A schematic of the gate driver topology is shown in Fig. 4.4. The floating gate driver implementation is motivated by several factors: First, it is possible to use CMOS based drivers to switch the GaN-HEMT, since a voltage swing of only up to 5 V is required. This allows the use of efficient, low cost and fast CMOS based ICs. The low voltage swing required by the gate driver allows for faster switching since the rise and fall time is, assuming a constant slew rate, faster for a lower voltage swing. A second and very important benefit is that the gate driver circuit is fully independent of the discrete voltage levels used for each switching stage (i.e., V_1 to V_4 in Fig. 4.1). If a driver with reference to system ground is implemented for a system as shown in Fig. 4.1 (b), the required output voltage of the driver for transistor T_4 is $G_4 = V_{GS\_T4}+V_{OUT}$. Thereby, V_{GS_T4} is the gate-source voltage required to switch the transistor "on" or "off", but additionally the output voltage V_{OUT} must be added at the gate. This forces the gate driver design to take the output voltage and therefore the discrete supply voltages into account. For a multilevel modulator the gate driver design will become even more complex. A disadvantage of the digital isolators is the long propagation delay in the range of 5-10 ns. This makes the design not usable for a close-loop system since it would limit the bandwidth.

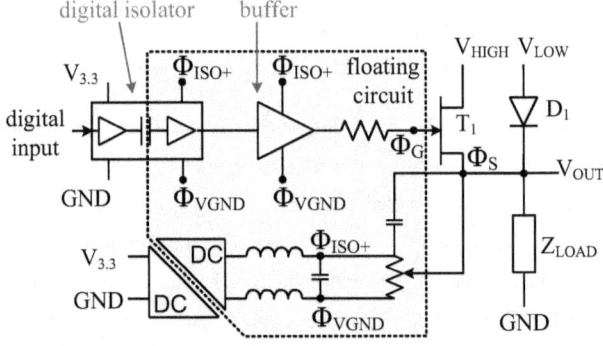

Fig. 4.4: Schematic of the galvanically isolated GaN-HEMT gate driver for normally-on n-type devices.

4.2.1 Digital Isolators

A digital isolator is a device that provides a galvanically isolated digital signal path. Compared to a simple optocoupler the biggest advantage is, that digital isolators capable of operating at high sampling rates are available. For the design of class-G supply modulators for wideband modulated signals, short pulses and therefore high switching frequencies are required. Besides the fast switching capabilities, digital isolators are easy to implement in a system, since either LVCMOS or LVDS signals are used at the inputs and outputs, simplifying the integration into a system. The gate drivers developed in this work are based on two different devices. For the systems with lower switching speed requirements, a digital isolator from Silicon Laboratories, SI8620 [41], is used. Minimum pulse durations of 5 ns and switching frequencies up to 100 MHz were achieved with this device. The power consumption of the device is very low, making it suitable for low power class-G operation. The device provides a CMOS in- and output. For the high-speed systems with large modulation bandwidth (> 75 MHz), a digital isolator from Analog Devices, ADN4650 [42], is used. The device is designed to transmit two LVDS signals with up to 600 MS/s, i.e., pulse durations down to 1.7 ns. Compared to the SI8620 the device has a higher power consumption which makes it more useful in designs with high output power and multiple supply voltage levels, where both channels are utilized to design a multilevel gate driver.

Digital isolators allow very simple gate driver designs, but they also introduce some drawbacks in the system: First, as mentioned above, a large propagation delay in the range 5-10 ns is introduced. In a multi-input system, where the modulator is controlled by a digital source, the time alignment is not critical. For a single-input system, the control signal for the modulator must be extracted from e.g. the envelope of the modulated RF signal. In that case, the propagation delay is critical, since it requires the RF signal to be delayed as well, otherwise the system will operate asynchronously. A second disadvantage is the injection of additional jitter in the range of typically 150 to 350 ps (peak-to-peak) [41], [42]. Capacitive coupling between primary and secondary side was not seen to cause any problems.

4.2.2 Isolated DC/DC converters

The galvanically isolated gate driver requires an isolated power supply for its floating secondary side. For the first prototypes a commercial available device (Murata, CME0305) is used. For this device, however, it was observed that capacitive coupling between primary and secondary side becomes critical if the modulator switches at high frequencies. Therefore, a common-mode choke had to be used at the secondary side to suppress the distortions (see 4.2.3). Furthermore, the high quiescent power consumption of the device reduces the efficiency of the modulator for low output powers. To solve this problem, a low power isolated DC/DC converter was designed. The designed converter is an unregulated transformer-based DC/DC converter, operating at a fixed switching frequency of 420 kHz. A symmetrical transformer with three taps each on the primary and secondary side is used. The supply voltage is applied on the middle tap of the primary side. The lower and upper tap of the primary side are antiphase switched to ground with a 50% duty cycle. This induces a square wave signal on the secondary side, which is rectified by low forward voltage Schottky diodes and buffered by a capacitor. For the systems that require a stabilized voltage, a linear regulator is applied. The designed converter has a quiescent power consumption of only 24 mW while the commercial product consumes 170 mW. Depending on the transformer used, it is possible to generate multiple supply voltage levels on the secondary side as shown by the schematic in Fig. 4.5. The lower voltage (V_{OUT_2}) can be used to supply the secondary side of the digital isolator and any logic applied, while the higher voltage (V_{OUT_1} and V_{OUT_2} in series) can be used to power the gate driver final stage with a higher voltage. This allows minimization of the dissipated power which becomes more significant, if the average RF output power of the class-G system is reduced, as it is done when going towards higher RF frequencies. Fig. 4.6 shows different implementations for the secondary side of the DC/DC converter, based on the dual supply implementation shown in Fig. 4.5.

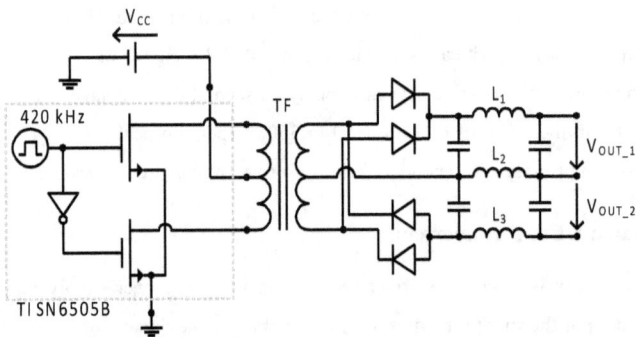

Fig. 4.5: Schematic of the isolated DC/DC converter with low quiescent current and two isolated output voltages (V_{OUT_1}, V_{OUT_2}).

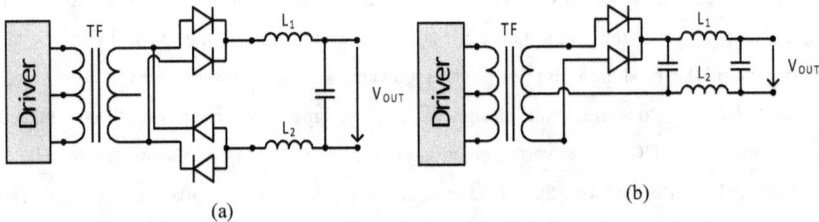

Fig. 4.6: Schematic of different single output configurations for the isolated DC/DC converter. Implementation for voltage transformation ratio (a) 1:2 and (b) 1:1.

The isolated DC/DC converter as shown in Fig. 4.5 is evaluated in the following. Therefore, power sweeps at the secondary side are conducted to evaluate the efficiency, the output voltage stability and the effect of asymmetric loading of the two isolated DC voltages (V_{OUT_1} and V_{OUT_2}). The transformer (TF) is driven by a rectangular input signal. This allows the DC/DC converter to show a relative stable output voltage without the use of any regulation. The results for the efficiency, power consumption and output voltage as a function of the output power are shown in Fig. 4.7 (a) to (d) for an unregulated output. For most of the output power range the total efficiency is 80%. The DC/DC converter delivers up to 400 mW output power on each of its outputs. The output voltage variation as function of the output power shown in Fig. 4.7 (c) and (d) exhibits only low variations for changing output power, especially a low interdependence between both outputs is visible.

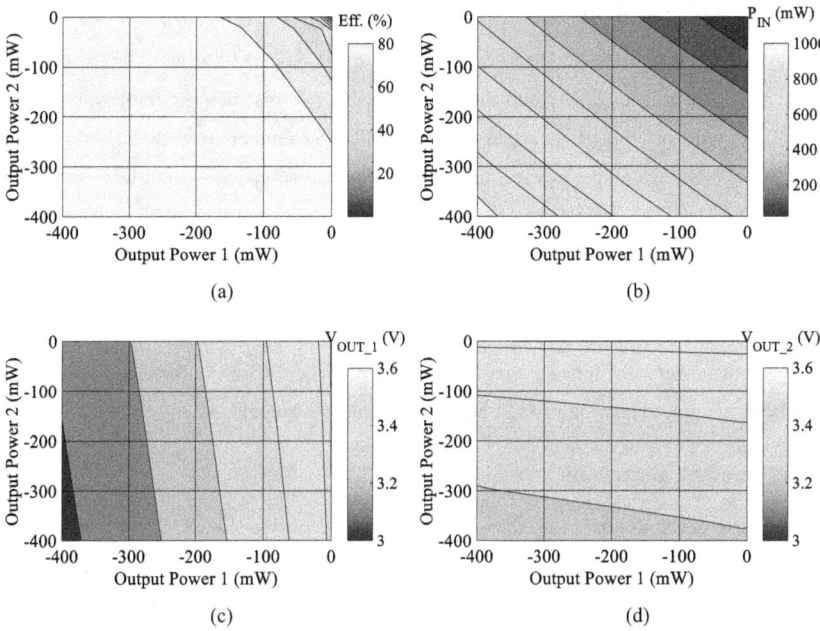

Fig. 4.7: Measurement results for the isolated DC/DC converter with two separate output voltages operated with a single 3.7 V input voltage; (a) efficiency, (b) input power and (c), (d) output voltage as a function of the output power.

4.2.3 Common-mode suppression

The secondary side of the galvanically isolated gate driver circuitry is referenced to the source potential of the transistor it is driving. Depending on the architecture of the switching stage, the voltage between the source terminal and system ground can be equivalent to the modulator output voltage, e.g. as shown in Fig. 4.1 (b). At the interface between the primary and secondary side of the isolated gate driver, this results in a common-mode voltage drop across the galvanic isolation. The common-mode voltage can cause high currents that can disturb the operation of the gate driver due to parasitic coupling. Especially in transformer-based isolated DC/DC converters, the tight coupling between primary and secondary side results in a capacitive coupling of the common-mode at higher frequencies, which was observed to cause pulse width distortions or even a full breakdown of the gate driver. For the digital isolator, only minor coupling was observed. Therefore, to ensure stable operation, a low-pass filter which also suppresses the common-mode is implemented in the isolated DC/DC converter path of the gate driver.

4.3 Class-G supply modulator designs

Several class-G modulators were designed and fabricated during this work. The modulators can be categorized into three generations. The first two generations consist of modulators with switching frequencies up to 100 MHz (5 ns minimum pulse duration) which provide high average output powers. In the first two generations, the gate driver circuits are almost identical. The second generation improves the multilevel capabilities of the first generation by a modular design based on printed circuit board (PCB)-edge connected switch-cards. The third generation uses a newly developed gate driver circuit and switches with frequencies up to 250 MHz (2 ns minimum pulse duration). It is designed to provide high peak output power but limited average output power. The design is also modular, but two transistors are placed on a single PCB-edge connected switch-card.

4.3.1 The first generation

The first generation of class-G modulators is based on the Si8620 digital isolator and commercial silicon Schottky diodes. A GaN-HEMT transistor mounted in a package with low thermal resistance is used. Two different modulator formats are designed, both based on the same isolated gate driver. The first design is a two-level modulator cell, which can be extended to a multilevel modulator by stacking of multiple modulators.

In the first prototype the digital isolator is connected externally and a separate isolated DC/DC supply is used. A photo of the modulator is shown in Fig. 4.8 (a). The floating gate driver is powered by an isolated 5 V supply ($V_{5.0\_ISO}$) which is implemented by a mobile phone charger. With this modulator, the first dynamically operated class-G prototype was successfully operated and published in [43]. Even though the modulator was not optimized, an instantaneous modulation bandwidth of 20 MHz with an efficiency improvement > 10% points was achieved. The good results motivated the isolated gate driver topology and an optimization of the modulator, leading to a revised design with the digital isolator and the isolated DC/DC supply integrated on a size-optimized board. A photo and schematic of the modulator are presented in Fig. 4.8 (a) and (b), respectively.

4 Class-G Supply Modulators

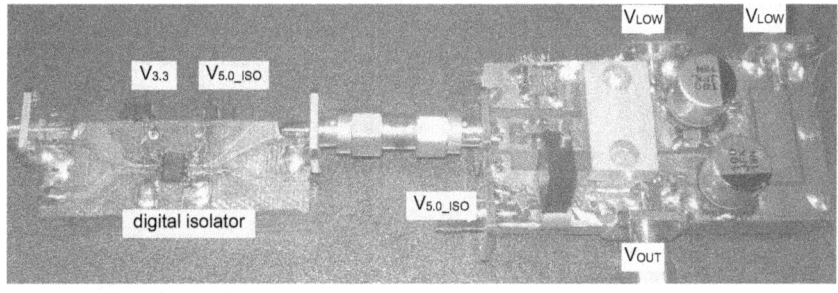

(a)

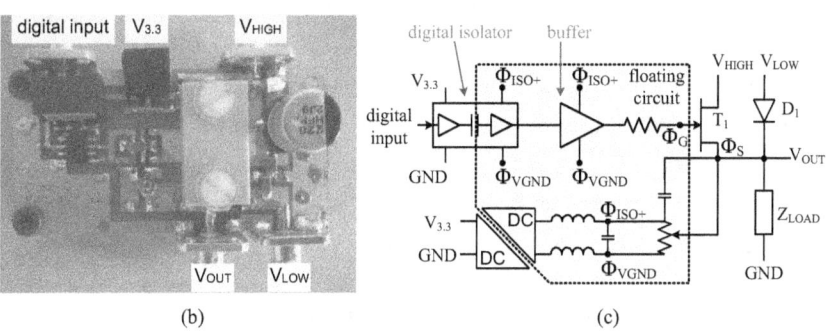

(b) (c)

Fig. 4.8: (a) Photo of the first two-level modulator prototype, and (b) photo of the revised size optimized design; (c) schematic of the first generation class-G modulator.

The revised modulator is characterized for switching frequencies up to 120 MHz and operates stable up to 100 MHz with high efficiency. For evaluation of the efficiency, a resistive probe was designed and characterized using a vector network analyzer (VNA). To evaluate different load impedances a dummy load consisting of different RF resistors was fabricated and characterized using a VNA. In combination with the S-Parameters of the resistive probe a two-port S-parameter dataset is generated. This allows the calculation of the power dissipation in the load based on voltage measurements using a digital sampling scope (DSO). The S-parameters of the RF loads seen by the modulator through the resistive probe (S_{11} at p_1) and the measurement setup for the characterization of the modulator are shown in Fig. 4.9 (a) and (b), respectively.

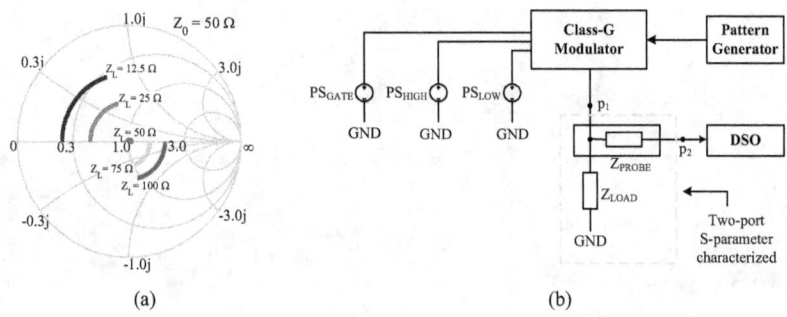

Fig. 4.9: (a) S-parameters of the different RF load impedances and (b) measurement setup for the characterization of the class-G modulator.

For the efficiency measurements the class-G modulator is driven with a 50% duty cycle signal. The switching frequency is swept in the range from DC to 120 MHz. The results for the switching stage efficiency and the system efficiency, i.e., the efficiency including the power dissipated in the gate driver, are shown in Fig. 4.10 (a) and (b), respectively. The efficiency at low switching frequency is dominated by the "on-resistance" of the GaN-HEMT and the diode and depends on the current level drawn by the load. For load impedances down to 25 Ω the efficiency at low frequencies is above 96.5%. For increased switching frequencies the efficiency decreases almost linearly, since the switching losses are proportional to the switching frequency.

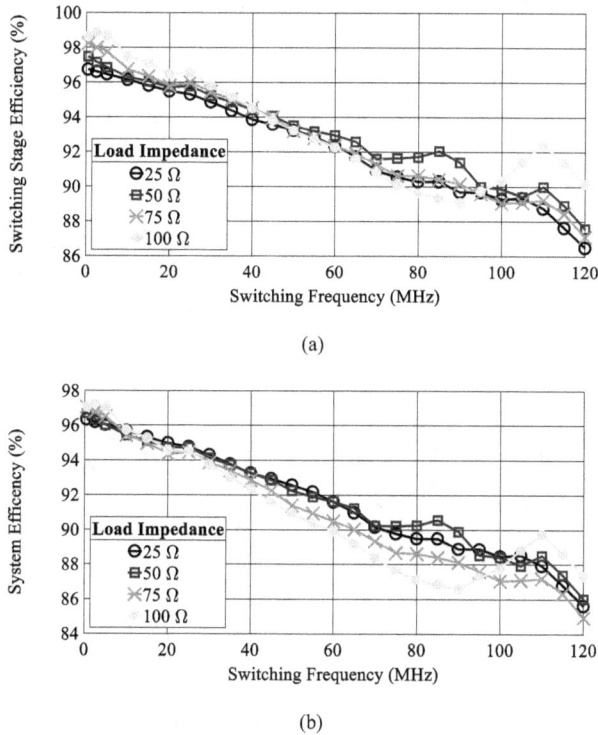

Fig. 4.10: Efficiency of (a) switching stage and (b) system against switching frequency for a 50% duty cycle signal.

4.3.2 The second generation

The first generation verified the concept of GaN-based class-G modulators with isolated gate drivers. In the second generation, the multilevel capabilities were improved. A very flexible modular design with reduced parasitic inductances between the single switching stages is introduced. In the first generation, cables connected to SMA-connectors were used to combine multiple modulators to a multilevel system. This introduced parasitic inductance in the frequency range of operation. The second modulator generation is based on a motherboard with connecters for PCB GaN-switch cards as shown in Fig. 4.11 (a). Two versions of the switch cards were developed, one with the same circuitry as the first-generation modulator and high average output power capabilities. In the first version, the isolated DC/DC converter is based on a commercial product, resulting in a quiescent power dissipation of 170 mW. The second version is a low quiescent power design with a custom isolated DC/DC converter design (see 4.2.2). Thereby the quiescent power consumption is reduced to only 24 mW, making it more useable in low power applications. This reduces the maximum power dissipation, but still allows high peak output powers. Furthermore, the size of the switch-card is reduced using SMD-packaged GaN-HEMT transistors. A photo of the switch-card is shown in Fig. 4.11 (b).

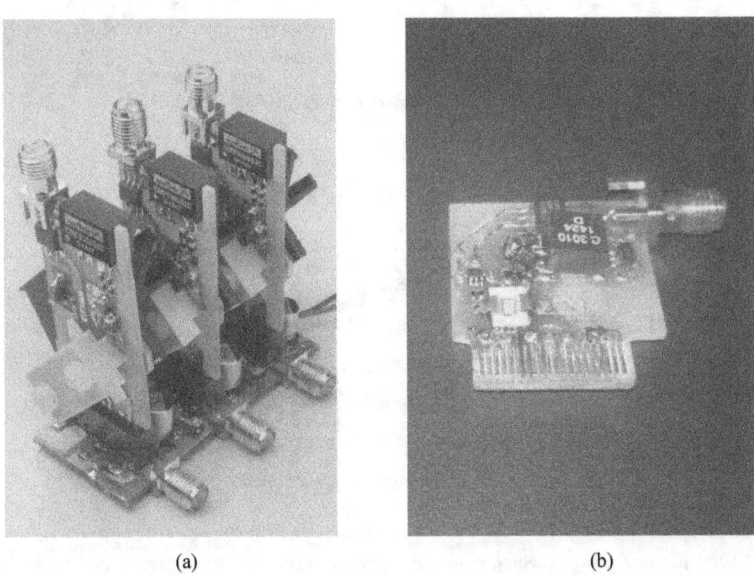

Fig. 4.11: Modulator motherboard with three high-power GaN-switch cards of the second modulator generation (a) and a low power GaN-switch card (b).

4.3.3 The third generation

In the first and second generation of class-G modulators, the minimum pulse duration was limited by the digital isolator and the Si Schottky diode. A solution therefore was found in a drop-in dual channel LVDS isolator from analog devices (ADN4650) which is specified for data rates of 600 MS/s, i.e., minimum pulse durations of ~1.7 ns. The Si Schottky diode was replaced by a GaN Schottky diode developed at the FBH. The significantly increased power consumption of the ADN4650 compared to the Si8620 motivated the utilization of both channels, to build a three-level modulator that allows higher efficiency improvement to compensate for the increased driver losses. Each channel of the digital isolator drives a separate transistor as shown in the schematic and block diagram in Fig. 4.12. With this modulator design, switching frequencies up to 250 MHz and minimum pulse durations of

2.5 ns are achieved, allowing IQ-modulation bandwidths up to 120 MHz with peak output powers above 75 W [44].

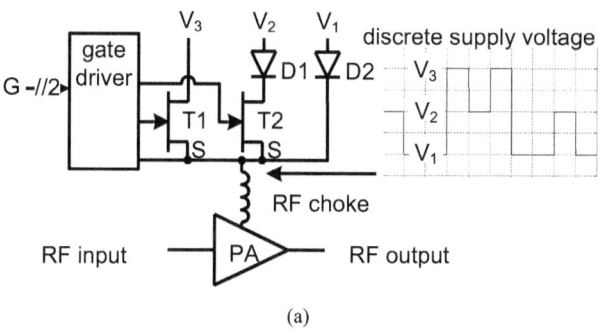

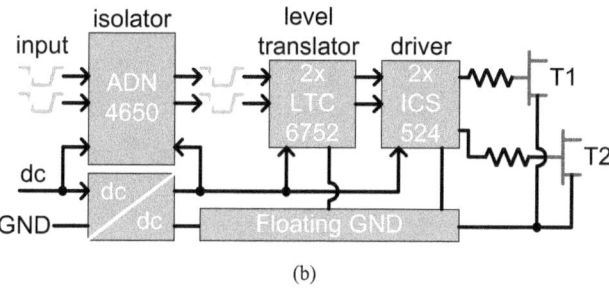

Fig. 4.12: (a) Block diagram of the third-generation modulator and (b) detailed gate-driver circuit.

5 Measurement Setup and Optimization

Most implementations of class-G PA systems are multi-input single-output systems. Multiple digital input signals are used to drive the class-G supply modulator, while the RF PA is driven by an IQ-modulated RF signal. For characterization of the linearity and efficiency, the RF output signal is measured using a vector-signal-analyzer or an IQ-demodulator connected to a DSO or digitizer combined with broadband RF power meters. The linearity is evaluated in the digital baseband. Therefore, the distortions inside the modulated band and the neighboring channels must be evaluated. The bandwidth of the measurement equipment should be three to five times higher than the IQ-modulation bandwidth of the test signal. For the high modulation bandwidth achieved with the class-G systems developed in this work (up to 120 MHz), a measurement setup based on discrete IQ-(de)modulators is implemented. The IQ baseband and the digital signals that drive the modulator are generated by a broadband arbitrary waveform generator (AWG). On the receiver side, a high-speed digitizer is used to sample the demodulated signal. Both, AWG and digitizer, are operated at a sampling rate of up to 2 GS/s and have a nominal resolution of 14 bit.

5.1 Multiple-input single-output setup for wideband modulated measurements

For the wideband measurements with multi-input signals a flexible but very complex measurement system was built. A block diagram is shown in Fig. 5.1. The key elements in the measurement setup are the wideband baseband signal generator and the signal analyzer. The signal generator provides two analog channels for the IQ-baseband signal and multiple digital output channels which are utilized depending on the amount of supply voltage levels implemented in the class-G modulators. Discrete IQ-(de)modulators are used as interface between the RF and baseband domain. Broadband RF couplers are applied to measure the available, reflected, and output power with power meters. A scalar calibration factor is applied for each power meter. For the calibration factor extraction, open/short measurements of the available and reflected power are performed. The attenuation introduced by the high-power attenuator and directional coupler on the output side is measured and used as calibration factor for the output power meter.

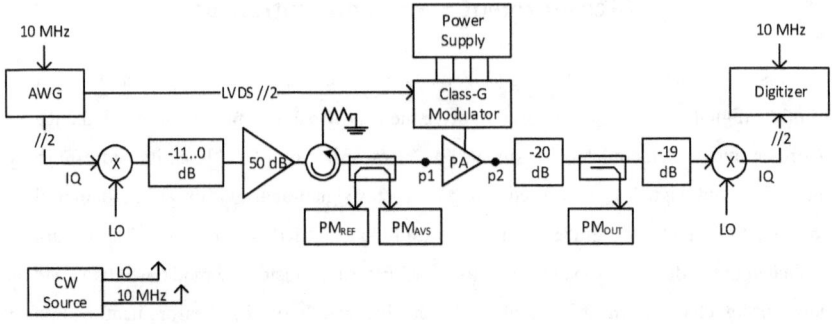

Fig. 5.1: Block diagram of the wideband multi-input measurement system. The ports p1 and p2 are calibrated references for CW power measurements.

5.2 Synchronization

In a measurement system for modulated signals, the synchronization of the measured signal with the original test signal is a crucial step that can degrade the accuracy if it is not properly implemented. A general requirement is the coherent operation of the waveform generator and -analyzer in the baseband frequency range. Coherency is ensured in the measurement system by a 10 MHz reference clock which is used to lock the sampling clocks on both devices. This ensures long term coherency of the waveforms. Since the modulated signals are repeated by the signal generator, it is only required to sample one or multiple periods of the original test signal. The PSD in the frequency domain can be evaluated directly while for the time domain evaluation the measured signal and the original test signal must be synchronized to allow a sample-to-sample based evaluation of the distortions. A simple possibility is using a marker output of the signal generator and a trigger input of the signal analyzer. This will produce synchronization with accuracy dependent on the trigger/marker implementation. The accuracy of this approach might not be sufficient for measurement systems used to implement and optimize digital predistortion algorithms. For signals continuously repeated by the signal generator, the accuracy of the synchronization can be improved with digital post-processing of the acquired data. A time domain synchronization based on the cross correlation of both signals allows a synchronization with the accuracy of one sample. For subsample accuracy, a correction of the linear phase shift in the frequency domain can applied.

A second and very important synchronization issue occurs in supply modulated systems where it must be ensured that the modulated supply voltage is synchronous with the modulated RF signal. This is crucial for high peak output powers and to achieve optimum efficiency improvement. If the synchronization is not accurate, it is possible that the RF PA is overdriven temporarily by the modulated RF signal if the supply voltage is below the targeted level. This will either degrade the linearity or require the reduction of the output power. The class-G systems implemented in this work are built as multi-input systems. The signal source is an AWG that generates analog and digital waveforms coherently. For the synchronization of the analog and digital channels, a synchronization routine is performed which calculates the misalignment based on the response of the RF PA gain when operated with supply modulation. The technique is based on the fact, that the implemented RF PAs show a supply voltage dependency of the gain which varies with up to 3 dB in a V_{DS} range from 20 V to 40 V. Once the time shift between the RF signal and the supply modulator output is calculated, a fixed offset is applied to the IQ-baseband signal prior to the upload to the AWG.

5.3 Dynamic range enhancement

The dynamic range (DR) of a measurement system defines the ratio of the lowest and the highest amplitude that can be measured. In a linear system without any noise the DR is dependent on the resolution of the digital-to-analog converter (DAC) in the signal generator and the analog-to-digital converter (ADC) in the digitizer/receiver. In a real system, nonlinearities and noise will degrade the dynamic range since distortions will mask the low amplitude levels. Therefore, the DR will be defined based on the signal-to-noise ratio (SNR) in the measurement system. In a digital system, the NMSE is an equivalent representation of the SNR based on time discretized signals. In [45] a linear relation between the change in effective number of bits (ENOB) and the NMSE for measurement systems with modulated signals is introduced:

$$\Delta ENOB = \frac{1 \text{ bit}}{6.02 \text{ dB}} \Delta NMSE$$
$$= \frac{1.66 \text{ bit}}{-10 \text{ dB}} \Delta NMSE \qquad (29)$$

The ENOB is used to describe the required resolution in bits that must be used by a perfect quantizer to reproduce the signal with an equivalent DR. The absolute ENOB for a defined NMSE is dependent on the PDF of the signal used. This is shown in Fig. 5.2 (a) for three signals with significantly different PAPR levels. Once the ENOB of the measurement system is measured it can be used to calculate the limitations of the measurement systems, e.g. the minimum achievable ACLR or NMSE for a given test signal.

Broadband measurement hardware with high dynamic range is an expensive investment. This motivates to exploit the maximum hardware capabilities of the measurement setup. For the enhancement of the DR two techniques are implemented. The first is oversampling of the signal, the second applies for periodical signals only and is based on averaging of multiple periods. Both techniques decrease the noise and also the NMSE if nonlinear distortions are not dominant. With oversampling, the quantization noise is spread over a wide frequency range which reduces the noise inside the frequency range of interest. The averaging of multiple signal periods maintains the signals power since the signals are correlated while the noise power is reduced. The possibility for oversampling is limited by the maximum sampling rate while periodically averaging is limited by the measurement time. The NMSE scales with the square root of the averaging factor (AVG) and the oversampling factor (OVS). Expressed in decibels, the change in NMSE is defined by:

$$\Delta NMSE_{AVG} = \log_2(AVG) \cdot 3 \text{ dB} \tag{30}$$

$$\Delta NMSE_{OVS} = \log_2(OVS) \cdot 3 \text{ dB} \tag{31}$$

Inserting (30) or (31) in (29) connects the change in ENOB with the AVS or OVS factor. According to the theory, an 1 bit increase in ENOB requires a four times higher AVS or OVS factor:

$$\Delta ENOB = 1 \text{ bit} \cdot (\log_4(AVG) + \log_4(OVS)) \tag{32}$$

A comparison of the theoretical ENOB improvement with the measured improvement achieved in a real system is shown in Fig. 5.2 (b). Accordingly, the measurement system achieves an ENOB of ~6 bit without any DR enhancement. For low AVG and OVS factors the improvement is close to the theory, but the oversampling-based improvement saturates at a factor of approx. 20, which represents a sampling rate of 2 GS/s. The DR improvement based on averaging does not show saturation in the measured range with an AVG factor up to 800. More details on the signals used and measurement hardware are given in [45].

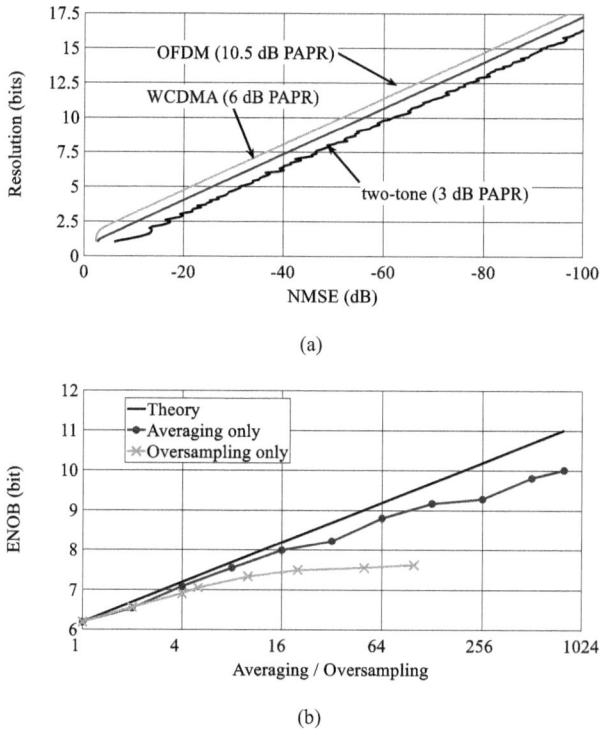

Fig. 5.2: (a) Relationship between ENOB and NMSE for different signal types and (b) ENOB improvement as function of the averaging and oversampling factor for measurements and theory.

6 Digital Predistortion and Signal Processing for Class-G Power Amplifier Systems

Power amplifiers based on GaN-HEMT technology exhibit a supply voltage dependency in the in- and output impedance. This causes a frequency shift of the PA operation band with the supply voltage. Another effect seen is the supply voltage dependency of the gain, e.g., the amplitude of the PA gain drops with decreasing supply voltages and its phase is shifted. Both effects cause distortion of the output signal when operating the PA with a modulated signal. Thereby, the linearity is degraded already for low output power levels below the gain compression and must be improved to meet the required specifications. A flexible way for improving the linearity is the use of baseband DPD. In this approach, the baseband processor applies an inverse model of the PA which predistorts the modulated baseband signal prior to the digital-to-analog conversion. For static supply PAs, predistorter models based on reduced Volterra series are widely used. They can compensate the nonlinearities and memory effects of the PA. The DPD becomes more complex for class-G modulated systems, since the gain and phase are not continuous with output power. Therefore, optimized predistorter models for class-G systems were developed, which will be presented in the following.

6.1 Baseband digital predistortion

If a modulated signal passes a nonlinear system, e.g., a RF PA, new frequency components will appear in the output spectrum. They are concentrated at multiples of the LO frequency and caused by intermodulation (IM). Despite that, the frequency components inside the modulation band will also be affected by IM distortions. A mathematical expression for this effect can be derived by approximating the nonlinear function $y(t) = f(x(t))$, $\mathbb{R} \rightarrow \mathbb{R}$, $x \mapsto y$, using a polynomial of order N

$$y(t) = \sum_{n=0}^{N} a_n \cdot x(t)^n \qquad (33)$$

and the modulated RF signal $x(t)$ defined by

$$x(t) = \operatorname{Re}\left\{\underline{x_{BB}}(t) \cdot e^{j \cdot 2 \cdot \pi \cdot f_0 \cdot t}\right\} \qquad (34)$$

6 Digital Predistortion and Signal Processing for Class-G Power Amplifier Systems

with the complex-valued modulated baseband signal $\underline{x}_{BB}(t)$ at the carrier frequency f_0. Inserting (34) in (33) delivers the expression of the distorted output waveform containing all frequency components:

$$\begin{aligned} y(t) &= \sum_{n=0}^{N} a_n \cdot \left(\text{Re}\left\{ \underline{x}_{BB}(t) \cdot e^{j \cdot 2 \cdot \pi \cdot f_0 \cdot t} \right\} \right)^n \\ &= \sum_{n=0}^{N} a_n \cdot \left(\text{Re}\left\{ \underline{x}_{BB}(t) \right\} \cdot \cos(2\pi f_0 t) + \text{Im}\left\{ \underline{x}_{BB}(t) \right\} \cdot \sin(2\pi f_0 t) \right)^n \end{aligned} \quad (35)$$

In mobile communication systems, linear amplification is required to avoid interferences of neighboring channels, and to achieve a high SNR which is required for modulation formats with high spectral efficiency. The suppression of the far out-of-band emission is less critical and can be realized by a band-pass filter. The in-band and adjacent channel region will still suffer from distortions caused by nonlinearities. To compensate them, predistortion techniques are applied to the input signal of the transmitter. Baseband digital predistortion is a complexity-optimized predistortion technique that only characterizes and corrects for the distortions located close to the carrier frequency. This allows the processing of the predistortion at the baseband sampling rate and a systematic complexity reduction in the mathematical models used for the predistorter. Fig. 6.1 shows the PSD of a modulated signal which is distorted by a nonlinear system. The marked frequency range shows the information which is sampled by the baseband receiver and used for DPD. All other frequency components are removed by a filter and not visible in the baseband. As a result, only odd order IM products are sampled in the baseband (see Appendix 9.2). With this pre-knowledge, the complexity of the predistorter, e.g., behavioral models (see Chapter 6.4), can be reduced to model only odd order terms.

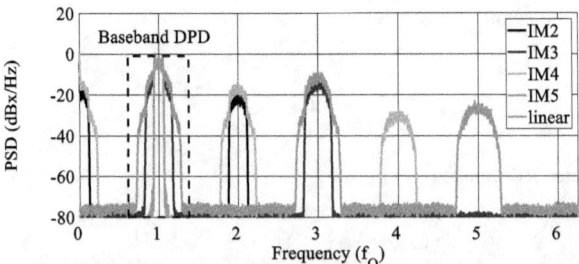

Fig. 6.1: Power spectral density of a modulated RF signal and spectral regrowth/intermodulation products caused by a nonlinear system.

6.2 Peak-to-average power reduction

Modulated signals based on OFDM modulation exhibit high PAPR values which can exceed 10 dB for a single symbol vector. Furthermore, it is observed that the PAPR of different symbols might vary strongly. For the design of a PA, the signal dynamics have to be constrained, otherwise a too large power-back off would be required to cover all possible PAPR levels and the degradation of average output power and efficiency would be severe. An OFDM symbol consists of multiple carriers with frequencies that are multiples of the symbol rate to ensure orthogonality. The maximum PAPR as function of the number of complex valued carriers (N) is defined as follows:

$$\begin{aligned} \text{PAPR} &= 10 \cdot \log_{10}\left(\frac{(N \cdot \hat{a})^2}{N \cdot \hat{a}^2}\right) \\ &= 10 \cdot \log_{10}(N) \end{aligned} \qquad (36)$$

It is shown that the PAPR is increased with N because the peak-power scales with N^2 while the average power scales with N. An OFDM modulated signal with 4086 carriers exhibits a theoretical maximum PAPR of 36 dB which can occur if all carriers are modulated with the same value. In practice the PAPR is below the theoretically derived limit since it would result in an uneconomic design. Fig. 6.2 shows a complementary cumulative distribution function (CCDF) derived from a dataset of 10.000 random payload OFDM symbols, generated in MATLAB. In (a) different number of active carriers and (b) different inverse discrete Fourier transformation (IDFT) lengths are shown. The carriers are modulated with binary phase-shift keying (BPSK) and have constant power levels. It is shown that the number of active carriers has an impact on the signal PAPR. The IDFT length itself shows only minor impact on the PAPR distribution. Only for an IDFT length close to the number of active carriers (IDFT 256), frequency components close to the Nyquist frequency are generated and an influence on the PAPR distribution is observed, since the time domain resolution in the digital baseband signal is too low and the peak value might be between two samples. Therefore, it is suggested to process the baseband signal with a relative IQ-modulation bandwidth (B/f_S) below 0.5, with f_S being the baseband sampling frequency.

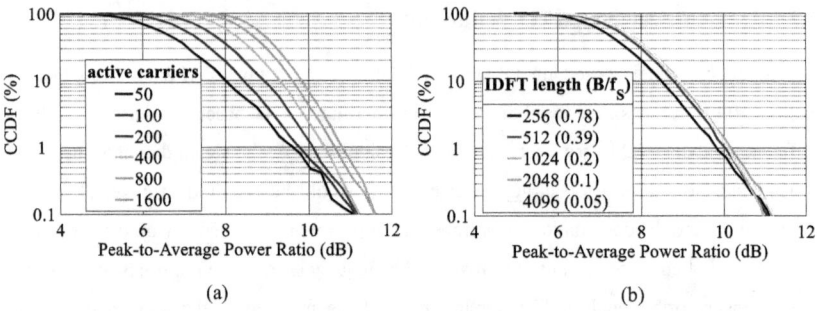

(a)　　　　　　　　　　　　　　(b)

Fig. 6.2: CCDF function for OFDM modulated signals with BPSK modulated subcarriers with (a) constant IFFT length of 4096 and changing number of modulated subcarriers and (b) 200 modulated subcarriers and different IFFT lengths. Dataset based on 10.000 symbols with random payload data.

The low spectral efficiency of BPSK modulation motivates the use of modulation schemes like quadrature amplitude modulation (QAM). QAM is widely used and achieves higher data rates than BPSK without increasing the modulation bandwidth but requires a smaller EVM. The CCDF for a 4-QAM and 16-QAM modulation for an IDFT length of 4096 is shown in Fig. 6.3 (a) and (b), respectively. The simulation shows that the modulation scheme used for the subcarriers is influencing the PAPR of the signal. Especially if amplitude modulation is applied to the active carriers, i.e., as for 16-QAM, the average power per symbol (one IDFT vector) can change and additional dynamics are added to the time domain signal.

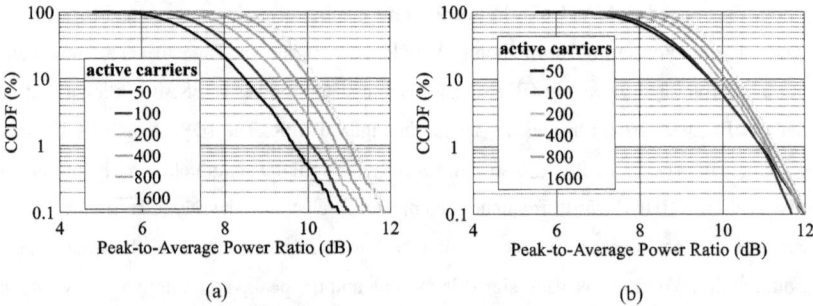

(a)　　　　　　　　　　　　　　(b)

Fig. 6.3: CCDF for OFDM modulated signals with constant IFFT length of 4096 and changing number of modulated subcarriers. (a) 4-QAM and (b) 16-QAM modulated subcarriers. Dataset based on 10.000 symbols with random payload data.

Under the assumption that no PAPR reduction is applied, the PA must be operated in power back-off according to the CCDF of the signal PAPR to ensure that the peak power levels are amplified properly. If a DPD linearization algorithm is applied, convergence problems can occur if the peak power levels are clipped due to PA overdrive. This is caused

6 Digital Predistortion and Signal Processing for Class-G Power Amplifier Systems

by the behavior of the algorithm DPD, which emphasizes the input amplitude of samples where the amplitudes at the PA output are compressed. If PAPR reduction is applied to the signal and the DPD is applied on the PAPR reduced signal, stable operation is achieved.

The CCDF distributions show that OFDM modulated signals cover a wide PAPR range. Depending on the ACLR and EVM requirements it is possible to reduce the PAPR of a signal to a certain level until the distortions introduced by the PAPR reduction reach the specified limit. The fact that a QAM modulation with higher spectral efficiency requires a lower EVM to achieve the same bit error ratio allows less PAPR reduction. In combination with the observed inherently higher PAPR of such a signal the required power back-off will be significantly higher compared to, e.g., BPSK modulation.

PAPR reduction can be implemented in multiple ways. A method with low computational complexity is hard clipping of the amplitudes of the complex valued baseband samples and preservation of the phase angle. With z as the threshold level the clipping function is defined as follows:

$$\underline{y} = \begin{cases} \underline{x} & , |\underline{x}| < z \\ z \cdot \exp(1i * \arg(\underline{x})), & \text{else} \end{cases} \quad (37)$$

An exemplary amplitude distortion (AM/AM) and phase distortion (AM/PM) plot of the clipping function is shown in Fig. 6.4. As can be seen, the phase is unaffected by the clipping function.

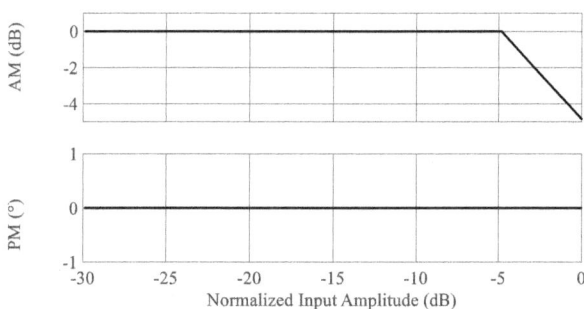

Fig. 6.4: AM/AM and AM/PM distortion caused by the hard clipping PAPR reduction routine for a reduction of 5 dB.

The impact of PAPR reduction on an OFDM modulated signal, consisting of 200 subcarriers modulated with 64–QAM is analyzed in the following. Fig. 6.5 shows the PSD of the OFDM signal for different levels of PAPR reduction. The corresponding amplitude CDF is shown in Fig. 6.6. A PAPR reduction to 5 dB already causes an increase in ACLR to ~ −30 dB. Based on the amplitude CDF it is seen, that only 5% of the signal is affected by the PAPR reduction in this case. With a lower level of PAPR reduction, less samples of the signal are affected resulting in a lower ACLR degradation.

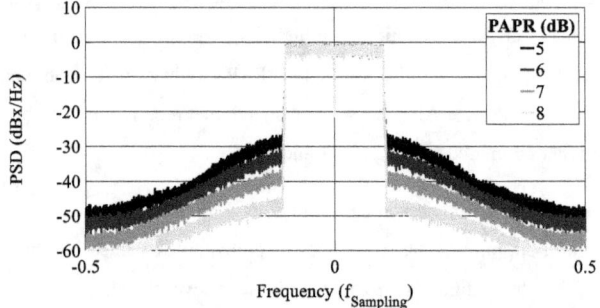

Fig. 6.5: PSD of the OFDM signal for different levels of PAPR reduction.

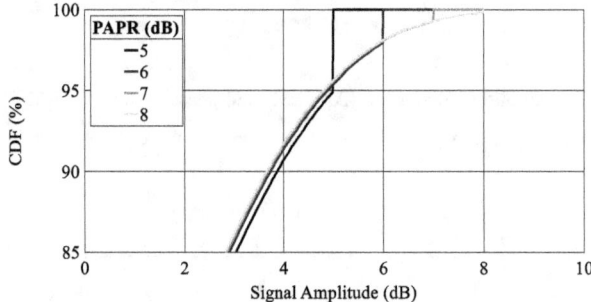

Fig. 6.6: Amplitude CDF of the OFDM signal for different levels of PAPR reduction.

The impact of PAPR reduction on the EVM is analyzed in Fig. 6.7 (a) to (d). The constellation diagrams of the 64-QAM modulated subcarriers are shown for a PAPR of (a) 5 dB up to (d) 8 dB. A PAPR reduction down to 7 dB (c) results in an EVM of 2.9%, which is the limit at the PA output for the 64-QAM modulation according to [46].

6 Digital Predistortion and Signal Processing for Class-G Power Amplifier Systems

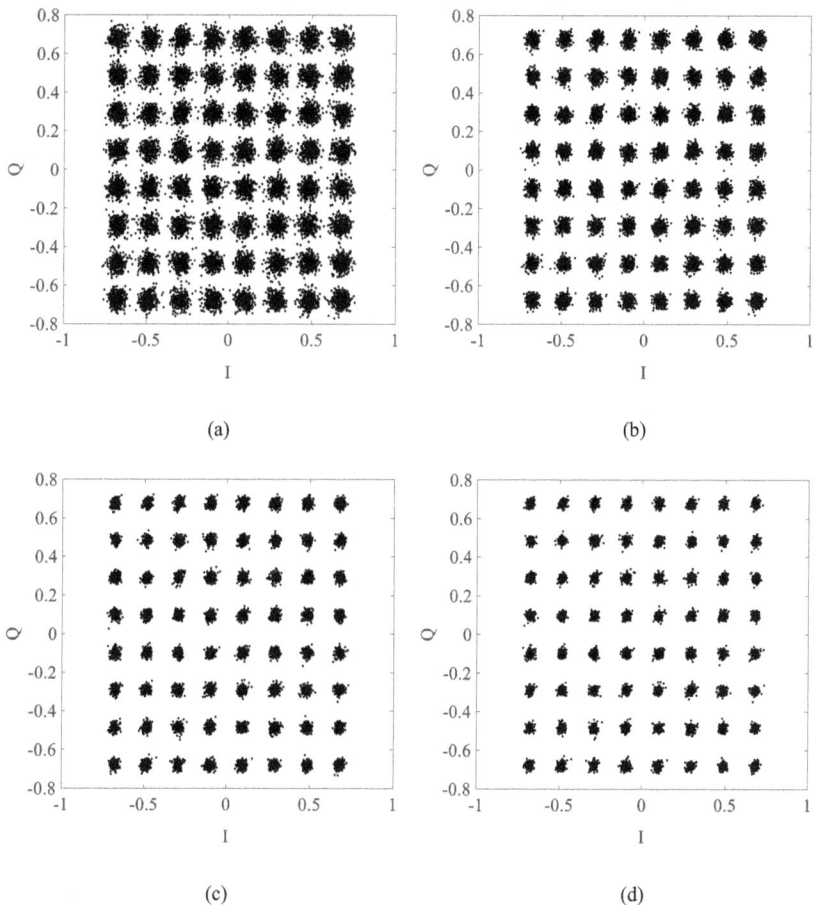

Fig. 6.7: Constellation diagram of the 64-QAM modulated subcarriers for the OFDM modulated signal with different levels of PAPR reduction: (a) PAPR = 5 dB and EVM = 6.2%, (b) PAPR = 6 dB and EVM = 4.0%, (c) PAPR = 7 dB and EVM = 2.9%, (d) PAPR = 8 dB and EVM = 2.4%.

This shows that a simple PAPR reduction technique already is a powerful tool that allows to trade linearity vs. average output power in a controlled way [47]. With the combination of clipping and filtering it is possible to reduce the ACLR distortions caused by the PAPR reduction at the cost of in-band nonlinearities [48].

6.3 Iterative learning control

The iterative learning control (ILC) algorithm is used to control repetitive processes [49]. Since most DPD measurements use periodical test signals, ILC can be applied for linearization of such signals. Recently it has gained attraction in the field of baseband DPD for RF PAs [44], [45], [50] and [51]. The advantage of ILC is that no PA specific model is required for predistortion of the test signal. With ILC linearization, for each sample a separate correction coefficient is calculated and optimized iteratively. With $\underline{y_i}$ being the measured signal at the output of the nonlinear system, $\underline{x_1}$ being the input signal and the iteration index i the ILC algorithm is performed as follows

$$\underline{y_i} = f(\underline{x_i}) \qquad (38)$$

The input signal x_i is then calculated based on (39) with $k \in \mathbb{R}^+$ being the gain factor that scales the error signal and controls the convergence characteristics.

$$\underline{x_{i+1}} = \underline{x_i} + k \cdot \left(\underline{x_1} - \underline{y_i}\right) \qquad (39)$$

If the process is stable, then y_i will converge to x_1. A major drawback of the ILC based predistortion is that the parameters are only valid for the dataset used for extraction, i.e., it cannot be used with a signal that is non-periodic and changing over time. Since this is valid for almost all communication systems that are used for data transmission, another linearization algorithm must be used in this case.

6.4 Behavioral model based digital predistortion

This digital predistortion technique is used to generate a predistorter that, contrary to an ILC based predistortion, accepts non-periodic signals. For this purpose, the PA is characterized, and an inverse model of the nonlinear behavior is constructed and used to process the predistorted signal. Several different predistorter model architectures were developed in the past with different accuracy and complexity. Most models are based on complexity reduced Volterra series or rational functions. In this work, Volterra-based models are used and selected standard models are presented in the following.

6.4.1 Volterra-based models

Volterra series can be used to approximate nonlinear functions, based on polynomials as it like a Taylor series. Compared to Taylor series, the Volterra series can also model functions with memory effects by incorporating previous samples. In (40) a time discrete truncated Volterra series for a causal system with a memory depth of M samples and a nonlinear order of P is shown.

$$\underline{y}(n) = h_0 +$$

$$\sum_{n_1=0}^{M} h_1(n_1) \cdot \underline{x}(n-n_1) +$$

$$\sum_{n_1=0}^{M} \sum_{n_2=0}^{M} h_2(n_1, n_2) \cdot \underline{x}(n-n_1) \cdot \underline{x}(n-n_2) + \ldots + \quad (40)$$

$$\sum_{n_1=0}^{M} \ldots \sum_{n_P=0}^{M} h_M(n_1, \ldots, n_P) \cdot \underline{x}(n-n_1) \cdot \underline{x}(n-n_2) \ldots \underline{x}(n-n_P)$$

The Volterra series as shown is very general and not optimized for a predistorter of a nonlinear PA, since it would result in a very complex model with too many parameters. The systematic complexity reduction of the Volterra series allows the creation of application specific predistorters. Two widely used and established predistorters are introduced in the following: The parallel Hammerstein (PH) and the generalized memory polynomial (GMP) [52]. Both models are capable of modelling memory effects by using multiple finite impulse response (FIR) filters. Memoryless models are not treated in this work, but can be derived from the models discussed by setting the memory depth to zero.

The parallel Hammerstein model (41) is a widely used model with a simple structure. It only models the odd-order nonlinearities and no cross-memory effects. The nonlinear order and the memory depth are defined by the parameters P and M, respectively. The model can be split into parallel paths, each consisting of a static nonlinear element followed by a linear filter. The total amount of coefficients ($\alpha_{p,m}$) is defined by: $N_{PH} = (M+1) \cdot (P+1)/2$.

$$\underline{y}_{PH}(n) = \sum_{p=1}^{(P+1)/2} \sum_{m=0}^{M} \alpha_{p,m} \cdot \underline{x}(n-m) \cdot |\underline{x}(n-m)|^{2(p-1)} \quad (41)$$

Another Volterra based model is the GMP model (36) [53]. It provides an improved linearization performance at the cost of higher computational complexity. The parameters K(a,b,c) define the nonlinear order for the linear L(a,b,c) and cross M(b,c) memory terms. Both models, the parallel Hammerstein and the GMP, can be used to either model the nonlinear behavior of a PA or its predistorter.

$$\underline{y}_{GMP}(n) =$$

$$\sum_{k=0}^{Ka-1} \sum_{l=0}^{La-1} \alpha_{k,l} \cdot \underline{x}(n-l) \cdot |\underline{x}(n-l)|^k +$$

$$\sum_{k=1}^{Kb} \sum_{l=0}^{Lb-1} \sum_{m=1}^{Mb} \alpha_{k,l,m} \cdot \underline{x}(n-l) \cdot |\underline{x}(n-l-m)|^k + \quad (42)$$

$$\sum_{k=1}^{Kc-1} \sum_{l=0}^{Lc-1} \sum_{m=1}^{Mc} \alpha_{k,l,m} \cdot \underline{x}(n-l) \cdot |\underline{x}(n-l+m)|^k$$

6.4.2 Model optimization for class-G operation

Most predistorter models presented so far are designed to linearize nonlinear systems with a continuous transfer function. In class-G systems, the switching of the supply voltage between discrete levels introduces discontinuities in the amplitude and phase of the PA gain as shown by the AM/AM and AM/PM distortion in Fig. 6.8 (further details on the device under test are given in Chapter 7.2.1). Very low linearity improvements are achieved on such a PA if a single Volterra series is used as predistorter. A simple workaround is the use of separate predistorter coefficients or models for each supply voltage level. Thereby the discontinuity is removed by splitting the signal in multiple partially continuous transfer functions.

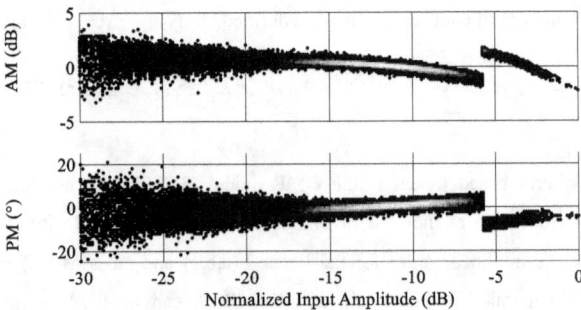

Fig. 6.8: Typical AM/AM and AM/PM characteristics of a GaN-based two-level class-G supply modulated PA at 2.65 GHz with 37 dBm average output power.

A suitable DPD model for this purpose is found in the vector switched model [54]. It implements a so called "vector switch" to select between different DPD models. If the input amplitude is used to control the vector switch, it can be setup to be synchronous with the supply switching thresholds which makes the VS model compatible with class-G systems.

A further improvement for class-G systems was developed in this work and presented in [55]. The improved model targets the transients in the supply switching region with an additional predistorter that works parallel to the VS predistorter as shown in the block diagram in Fig. 6.9.

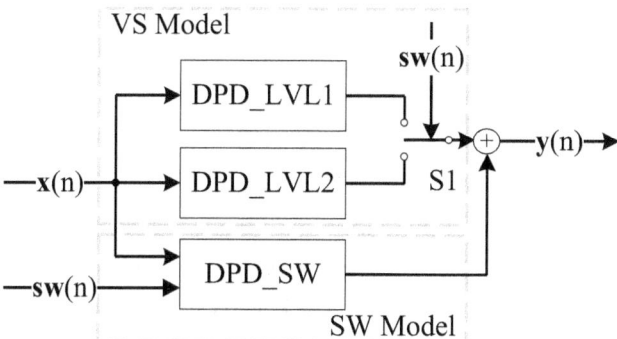

Fig. 6.9: Block diagram of the class-G optimized predistorter with compensation for supply voltage transients.

The DPD_SW model implements a static compensation polynomial in combination with filters to allow for correction of linear and nonlinear memory effects. The two predistorters in the VS model can be any behavioral model. For the following measurements the model proposed in [56] is used for both VS predistorters. The comparison of the AM/AM distortions after linearization with and without the class-G optimized model is shown in Fig. 6.10 for the transition region. The brightness of the points is related to the active supply voltage level. With the optimized model the distortions in the transition region are reduced significantly.

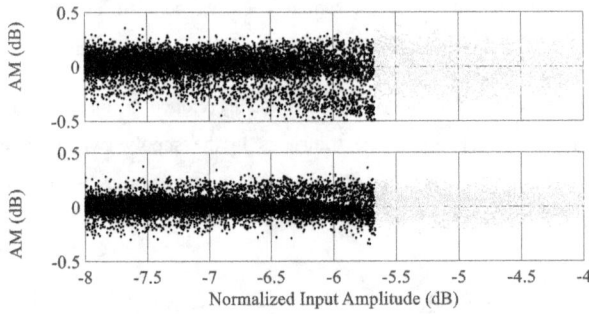

Fig. 6.10: AM/AM distortion after linearization (top) without and (bottom) with class-G optimized predistorter model, measured at 2.65 GHz with 35 dBm average output power.

6.4.3 Bandwidth requirements

Digital predistortion is used to compensate the nonlinear transfer function by applying an inverse nonlinear function. This function can be expressed as a polynomial with the order P. Hence, the digital predistortion causes the signal bandwidth to be expanded, depending on the order of the polynomial used. Since the data is processed in discrete-time, the highest frequency is limited, according to the Nyquist theorem, to half the sampling frequency f_s. With B as the IQ-modulation bandwidth the relative modulation bandwidth b is defined by

$$b = \frac{B}{f_s} \qquad (43)$$

Due to the nonlinear predistortion the bandwidth of the predistorted signal will be P times higher than b. With IQ-modulation, negative and positive frequencies in the baseband are possible and the frequency range is limited to $(-f_s/2, f_s/2)$. The maximum bandwidth is therefore $B = f_s$. Consequently the following condition must be fulfilled to avoid aliasing effects:

$$P < \frac{1}{b} \,^1 \qquad (44)$$

The constraint defined by (44) is hard to fulfill since it requires a bandwidth expansion of the baseband hardware compared to a system without DPD. A possible solution for elimination of aliasing effects is the use of different sampling rates for the signal processing

---

[1] The calculation is based on the assumption, that a complex valued signal is used which doubles the possible modulation bandwidth.

and the baseband sampling hardware: The signal is predistorted at a higher sampling rate followed by a low-pass filter and decimation. This allows the use of hardware with a lower sampling rate at the cost of computational complexity and possible degradations in linearity [57], [58].

6.5 Predistorter model training and coefficient extraction

Predistorter models represent a parametrized nonlinear function. Most models can be used to describe the nonlinear transfer function of a PA itself although they are used to model the inverse transfer function. A crucial step in the DPD procedure is the extraction of the model coefficients. The optimum predistorted signal is unknown which prohibits direct extraction of the coefficients. The most common implementation to overcome this is the iterative learning architecture (ILA). Thereby the model parameters are extracted in an iterative process. Another and very promising approach has been published recently and is based on ILC. Both algorithms are introduced in the following.

6.5.1 Model coefficient extraction

The behavioral DPD models can be expressed as a polynomial. To model a given nonlinearity the model parameters need to be defined which is done by a polynomial regression. The nonlinear function (45) represents a PA or its required predistorter and maps the input vector $\underline{x}$ (Nx1) to the output vector $\underline{y}$ (Nx1). The behavioral model approximates this function as shown in (46). Thereby $\underline{K}(x)$ is a (MxN) regression matrix that is generated according to the structure of the behavioral model and the input signal $\underline{x}$ and the parameter vector $\underline{a}$ (Nx1). For the extraction of $\underline{a}$, the regression matrix $\underline{K}(\underline{x})$ must be inverted (47). K is not invertible because it is not a regular matrix (M>>N). Therefore, the inversion must be approximated by calculation of a pseudo-inverse matrix. A possible expression for the pseudoinverse of $\underline{K}(\underline{x})$ is given by (48) with $\underline{K}(\underline{x})^+$ being the pseudo-inverse. It has the constraint that the column vectors of $\underline{K}(\underline{x})$ are linearly independent, which should be fulfilled for all complexity-optimized behavioral models. Formula (49) gives the full expression for the estimated parameter vector.

$$\underline{y} = f(\underline{x}) \qquad (45)$$

$$\underline{y} \cong \underline{\hat{y}} = \underline{K}(\underline{x}) \cdot \underline{a} \qquad (46)$$

$$\underline{K}'(\underline{x}) \cdot \underline{y} = \widehat{\underline{\alpha}} \qquad (47)$$

$$\underline{K}(\underline{x})^+ = \left(\underline{K}(\underline{x})^T \cdot \underline{K}(\underline{x})\right)' \cdot \underline{K}(\underline{x})^T \qquad (48)$$

$$\widehat{\underline{\alpha}} = \left(\underline{K}(\underline{x})^T \cdot \underline{K}(\underline{x})\right)' \cdot \underline{K}(\underline{x})^T \cdot \underline{y} \qquad (49)$$

6.5.2 Predistorter training based on iterative learning architecture

The behavioral models introduced in Chapter 6.4 are generic models that can be applied to various PA implementations and communication signals. It is required to define the coefficients to construct a predistorter for a specific PA and signal type. This process is called coefficient extraction and a key step in the linearization process which has a strong impact on the achievable PA linearity. For the coefficient extraction the ILA can be used. A block diagram of the ILA is shown in Fig. 6.11. The input signal $\underline{x}$ is the signal to be linearized and $\underline{y}$ the signal measured at the PA output. The predistorted signal $\underline{z}$ is fed into the nonlinear PA and is generated by the "DPD 1" block. The DPD 1 predistorter predistorts the signal $\underline{x}$ using the coefficients defined by $\underline{\alpha}_{i-1}$. The index i denotes the iteration. In the first iteration (i=1), $\underline{\alpha}_0$ is initialized so that $\underline{x}$ passes the predistorter without modification and $\underline{z}_0$ equals $\underline{x}$. In the following step the predistorter DPD 2 defines the coefficients $\underline{\alpha}_i$ to minimize the error signal $\underline{e}_i = \underline{z}_i - \underline{w}_i$ using the gain normalized measured output $\underline{y}_i$. It is important, that the predistorter models in both DPD blocks are identical, otherwise the parameters extracted in DPD 2 are not valid for DPD 1. In the following iteration (i+1), the DPD 1 block uses the coefficients extracted in the previous iteration ($\underline{\alpha}_i$) to calculate $\underline{z}_{i+1}$. The iterations must be continued until the error signal reaches a threshold level or converges to a minimum value.

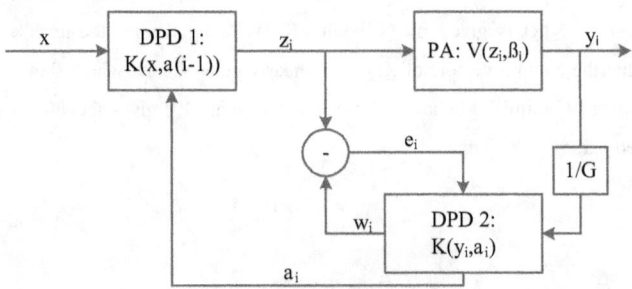

Fig. 6.11: Block diagram of the iterative learning architecture algorithm.

6.5.3 Predistorter training based on iterative learning control

The parameter extraction based on ILC offers some benefits over the ILA approach. With ILC the optimum predistorted signal $\underline{z}$ is extracted without the need for a predistorter model. This is achieved by linearizing the system using ILC as shown in Chapter 6.2. With the knowledge of the signal $\underline{z}$, it is possible to directly extract the model coefficients for any behavioral DPD model. This also allows off-line optimization of the behavioral model and comparison to other models. The ILC algorithm itself only requires simple mathematical operations which can contribute to lower power consumption during the parameter extraction phase.

7 Class-G RF Power Amplifier System Optimization

7.1 State-of-the-art

Class-G supply modulation is an efficiency enhancement technique that was initially introduced for high-power audio amplifiers. For RF systems it was considered only recently but minor attention was paid to this topic. Only few articles were published, mostly targeting low-power integrated solutions ([59]-[61]) where class-G might not exhibit its full advantages over continuous supply modulation techniques. The field of high-power class-G modulation with packaged GaN devices was almost untouched at the beginning of this work. In 2012 the first class-G system that shows a significant efficiency improvement with a RF PA based on a packaged GaN-HEMT was presented [62]. The minimum pulse-width of the two-level supply modulator used in that system was 100 ns and limited the modulation bandwidth. Furthermore, the linearity was degraded severely due to the lack of DPD linearization.

The systems developed in this work and presented in the following contribute significantly to the progress in the field of high-power class-G supply modulated RF PAs. The first prototype developed already presented the highest modulation bandwidth achieved at the time of publication and showed the first investigations on linearity and linearity improvement using digital predistortion. This was enabled mainly by the RF GaN-HEMT based class-G supply modulators which provide minimum pulse widths of less than 5 ns. The developed class-G systems managed to reach state-of-the-art efficiency results which compare well with continuous envelope tracking systems and even higher modulation bandwidths. A benchmarking of the class-G modules with state-of-the art efficiency enhanced PA solutions is given in Table 4. It shows that the class-G systems developed in this work (bold) achieve the best results for supply modulated systems (SM) in terms of PAPR, average output power (P_{OUT_AVG}) and PAE. Compared to Doherty PAs it is observed that the class-G supply modulation closes the gap but it is still less powerful in terms of instantaneous modulation bandwidth (IBW).

Table 4: State-of-the-art comparison to other efficiency enhanced systems for high PAPR signals. Class-G systems presented in this work are bold.

Ref.		[63]	[64]	[65]	[66]	[67]	[68]	[69]	[70]	[44]
Freq.	[GHz]	1.50	10	2.15	9.23	3.5	2.0	2.0	**1.85**	**1.80**
IBW	[MHz]	20	100	80	60	100	160	365	**20**	**120**
PAPR	[dB]	6.5	6.6	6.6	6.6	9.7	9.3	7.3	**9**	**10.0**
P_{OUT_AVG}	[dBm]	33.0	37.1	30.7	30.2	~35**	33.9	39.3	**40**	**39**
PAE	[%]	39.0	51.5	35.3	32.4	52.0	45.0 (DE)	43.5	**50.8**	**38.5**
ACLR	[dB]	−36.0	*	−45.1	*	−50.0	−47.0	−50.1	**−40.3**	**−46.5**
Type		SM	SM	SM	SM	Doherty	Doherty	Doherty	**SM**	**SM**
Year		2016	2015	2017	2013	2014	2016	2017	**2016**	**2017**

*: information not available
**: information derived from data in the paper

7.2 Milestone Class-G Systems

In this section the milestones in the development of competitive high-performance class-G supply modulated PA systems are summarized. Several systems were developed and evaluated during the course of this work. All systems use discrete packaged GaN-HEMTs for PA and modulator, with devices developed and fabricated at FBH. Design and realization follow the approaches described in the previous chapters.

7.2.1 40 W RF power amplifier based system operating at 2.65 GHz

The first class-G supply modulated PA prototype employed a GaN-HEMT with 10 mm total gate-width. The design frequency is set to 2.65 GHz, targeting the downlink channel of the E-UTRA band 7. The RF power amplifier matching- and stabilization networks are designed based on a Chalmers simulation model for the transistor. The evaluation of the PA using CW measurements revealed a mismatch in the IMN due to inaccuracies of the simulation model. Therefore, the PA was tuned manually to its desired operating frequency.

Hardware design

For the drain bias supply no a-priori knowledge on designing the interconnection between the class-G supply modulator and the RF power amplifier was available at beginning of this work. Therefore, the bias network was designed as a five-pole filter with a −1 dB cut-off frequency of 100 MHz, assuming a 20 Ω impedance system. The intention is to cover multiple times the targeted IQ-modulation bandwidth of 16 MHz to degrade the modulated supply voltage signal to a minimum extent. Since the RF PA does not provide a constant impedance at its drain bias terminal, the desired filter function cannot be maintained over the full supply voltage range, which motivated the high cut-off frequency.

The class-G modulator applied is the prototype version of the first generation of modulators. It uses the same RF GaN-HEMT as the RF PA. The design is not optimized in size and the digital isolator is implemented on a separate PCB. The two supply voltage levels can be chosen in the range from zero to 40 V.

A photo of the class-G supply modulator and the RF PA is shown in Fig. 7.1 (a) and (b), respectively.

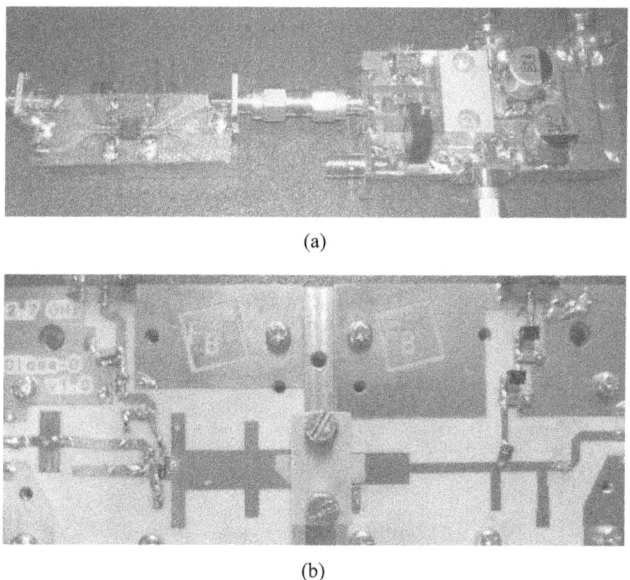

Fig. 7.1: Photo of the 40 W 2.65 GHz two-level class-G supply modulated PA system; (a) modulator and (b) RF PA board.

Measurements

For the dynamic evaluation of the class-G system, the two supply voltage levels are set to 20 V and 40 V. A 16 MHz OFDM modulated signal with a PAPR of 10.5 dB is applied. The class-G supply modulator is fed with a 100 MS/s serial bit pattern, generated by a multichannel 14 bit AWG (VB8000, YOKOGAWA), which is also used for generation of the

IQ-baseband signal. Therefore, the minimum pulse duration is limited to 10 ns by the measurement equipment. Compared to the operation with a single 40 V supply voltage, a PAE improvement of 10 to 15 percentage-points is achieved, which is shown in Fig. 7.2 (a). In the modulated class-G measurements the supply voltage is switched between 20 V and 40 V. The switching threshold level P_{TH} defines the threshold power level for supply switching, in relation to the average output power. For P_{TH*} the supply switching signal is treated specially. First, the waveform is calculated based on the threshold level of 2 dB, and then the pulses of high supply voltage are expanded by one sample (10 ns) at the beginning and end of each pulse. Linearity degradation for the operation with class-G supply modulation is observed for out-of-band emission as shown in Fig. 7.2 (b). The in-band distortions, quantified by the EVM in Fig. 7.2 (c), show a different behavior than observed for the ACLR. For $P_{TH} = 4$ dB, the EVM and ACLR are degraded equally over the full average output power range. If the threshold level is reduced, a larger EVM improvement is achieved at power back-off and the class-G system operates better than the PA operated with a fixed supply voltage.

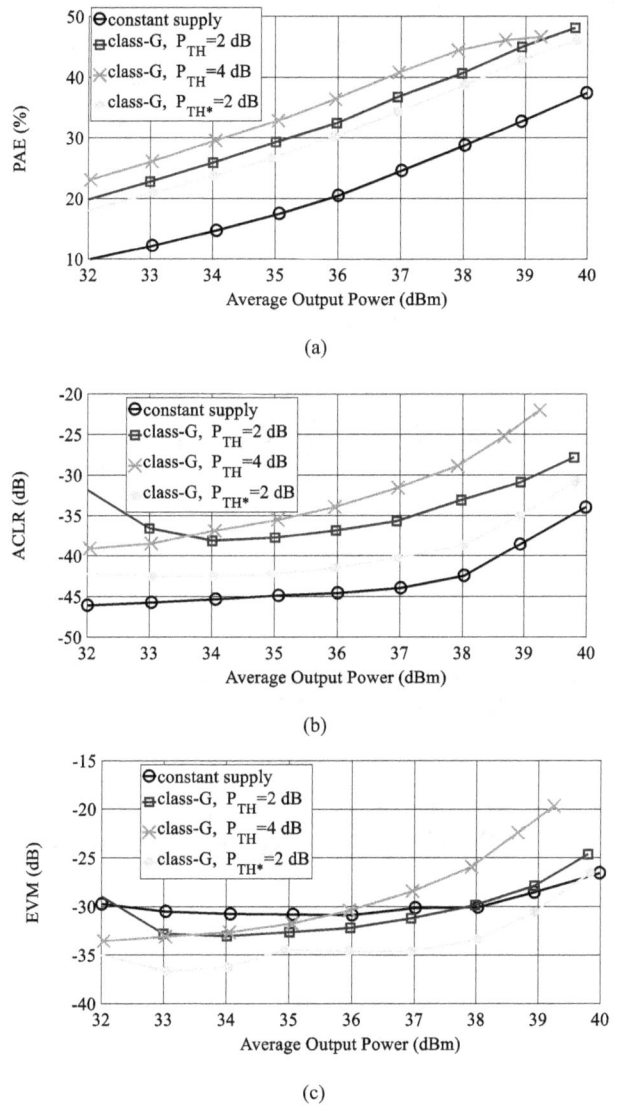

Fig. 7.2: Measurement results at 2.65 GHz: (a) PAE, (b) ACLR and (c) EVM vs. average output power for different supply voltage configurations with DPD linearization.

At the switching threshold level, the AM/AM and AM/PM characteristics in Fig. 7.2 (a) show a sharp discontinuity. Without DPD linearization this causes the output signal of the PA to be significantly distorted resulting in linearity degradation. The use of DPD allows removing the discontinuity although an increase in distortions located around the threshold level is still observed as shown in Fig. 7.3 (b). The abrupt change in amplitude and phase of the PA transducer gain reveals that the supply voltage switches its level fully within one sampling interval ($T_S = 10$ ns). This indicates that higher switching frequencies are possible with the class-G modulator, but the measurement system used for this investigation was already operated at its performance limit.

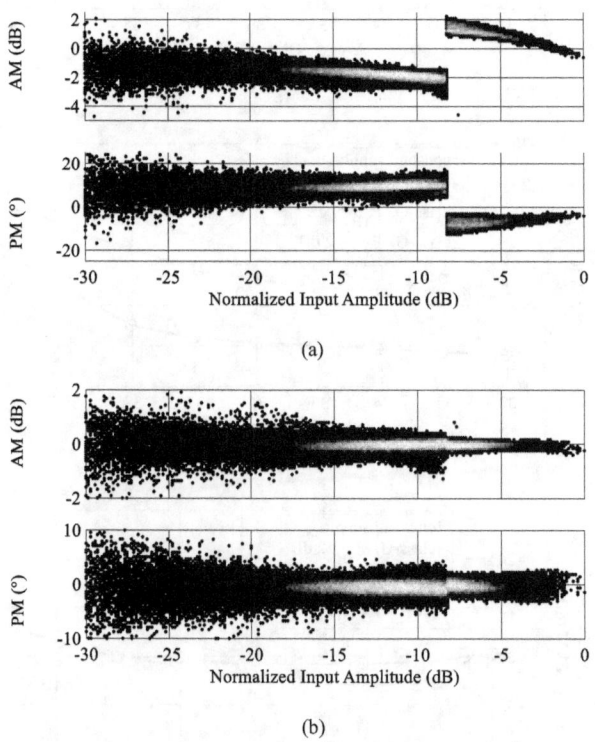

Fig. 7.3: AM/AM and AM/PM distortion (a) before and (b) after behavioral model based DPD linearization at 2.65 GHz with 36 dBm average output power.

Summary

This first design established an important basis for the following work and improvements on class-G supply modulated systems. It revealed the challenges for the DPD linearization of such systems but also the capabilities in high-efficiency operation with large modulation bandwidth and very high peak output power. The class-G system and the results were published in [43].

7.2.2 65W three-level class-G systems with over 50% PAE at 1.85 GHz and 20 MHz instantaneous modulation bandwidth

The design goal for this PA was to achieve an average PAE of 50% and a peak output power higher than 50 W for a wideband OFDM modulated signal. The realized system delivered the highest PAE achieved so far with class-G modulation on a 20 MHz modulated signal with a high PAPR of 9 dB. For the supply switching, a modulator of the second generation (see 4.3.2) employing two switch-cards is used. It features three discrete supply voltage levels. The PA is optimized for a frequency of 1.85 GHz and can be used in the full E-UTRA band 3.

Hardware design

For the PA design several major modifications were implemented to enhance the performance. The 10 mm GaN-HEMT transistor of the first design was replaced by a 16 mm device to achieve the desired goal of 50 W peak output power. A beneficial property of the device is the improved stability characteristics compared to the 10 mm device, which simplifies the stabilization network design. The operational frequency was reduced to 1.85 GHz where the device achieves a significant higher PAE compared to 2.65 GHz. Contrary to the first class-G system, the drain-bias path does not implement a filter function. It is reduced to an inductor-based RF-choke and a short transmission line that is directly routed to the connector for the supply modulator. This is an important modification that allows the use of shorter pulses of higher supply voltage, since the PA responds faster on the supply voltage variations. For the design of the matching networks load-pull measurements were used since the first design revealed that the available GaN-HEMT model is lacking accuracy when operated with supply modulation. The second and third harmonics at the output were matched to high reflection. The tuning of the phase angle was done manually by evaluating multiple output matching networks. A photo of the complete system is shown in Fig. 7.4.

Fig. 7.4: Picture of the 65 W 1.85 GHz three-level class-G supply modulated PA system.

Measurement results

The CW measurement results for the PA for three fixed supply voltage levels are shown in Fig. 7.5 for the saturated output power (a). The transducer power gain and PAE at saturated output power is shown in Fig. 7.5 (b) and (c), respectively. The frequency response of the PAE highlights the challenges in the design of a PA that operates efficiently over a large supply voltage range: The change in supply voltage influences the matching at the PA output and thus has a noteworthy influence on the PAE.

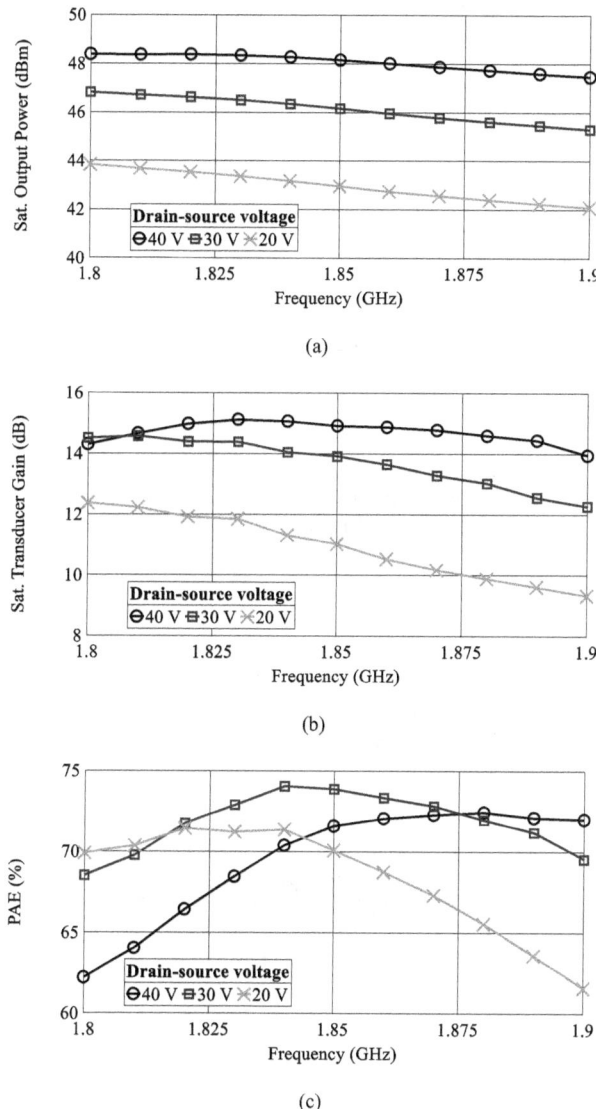

Fig. 7.5: Continuous wave frequency sweep of (a) saturated output power and corresponding (b) transducer power gain and (c) PAE for different supply voltage levels.

In dynamic operation this system reaches an outstanding PAE higher than 50% at an average output power of 40 dBm (10 W). Compared to single supply voltage operation, this is an improvement of over 18 percentage-points. In combination with DPD, an ACLR of less than -40 dB is achieved. Due to the three-level supply modulation the AM/AM and AM/PM characteristics in Fig. 7.6 (a) exhibit two discontinuities. Therefore, three separate behavioral models are used in the VS model to linearize each supply voltage region independently. The AM/AM and AM/PM distortion after DPD linearization is presented in Fig. 7.6 (b).

Finally, Fig. 7.7 shows the system PAE and the EVM and ACLR for different average output power settings. The threshold level for switching of the supply voltage is kept at a constant level during the power sweep.

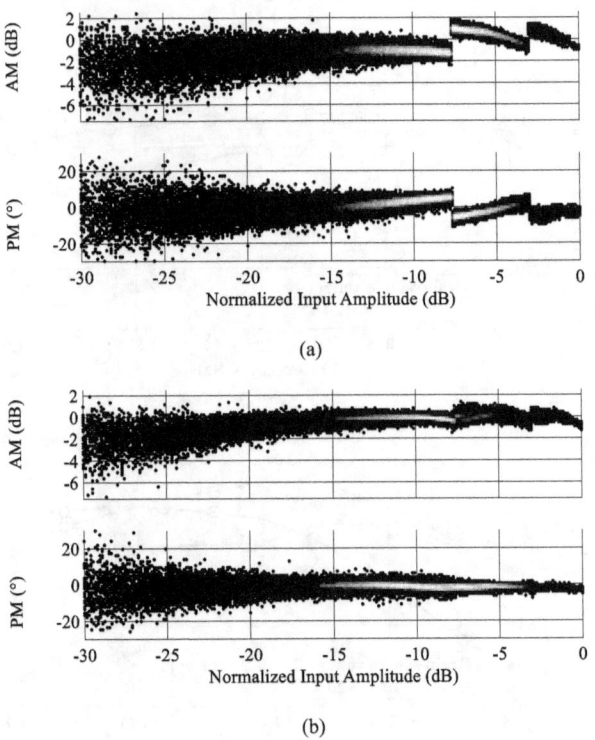

Fig. 7.6: AM/AM and AM/PM distortion at 1.85 GHz and 40 dBm average output power for a 20 MHz OFDM signal (a) without and (b) with VS behavioral model based DPD.

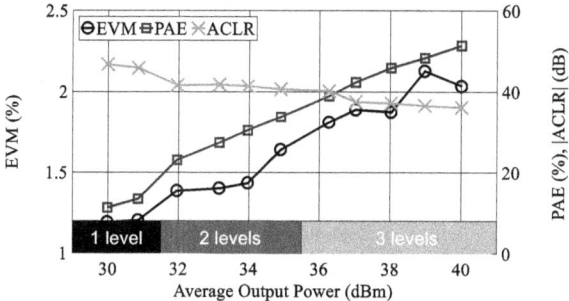

Fig. 7.7: Power sweep of the linearity and efficiency with fixed supply switching threshold levels.

The linearity under dynamic operation with DPD linearization depends on the performance of the measurement setup and the linearization method. The comparison of class-G operation with a VS behavioral model and an ILC algorithm is shown in Fig. 7.8. The fact that the ILC linearization achieves ~5 dB better ACLR underlines that the applied VS DPD model is still lacking accuracy.

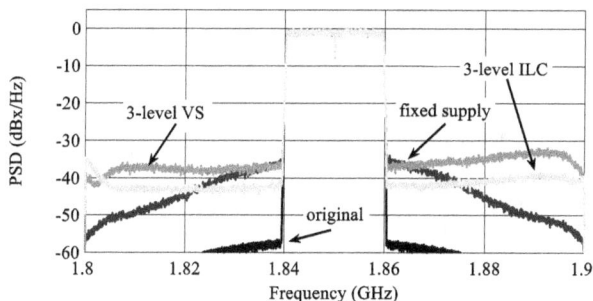

Fig. 7.8: Power spectral density of the linearized output signal for different DPD configurations at 40 dBm average output power at 1.85 GHz.

Summary

With the performance achieved by this system, class-G supply modulation has caught up with the high-efficiency continuous supply modulated state-of-the art. The results were published in [70].

7.2.3 Discrete-level gate bias and supply modulated PA

With the modulation of the supply voltage a significant efficiency improvement is achieved. A close look at the linearity of a class-G supply modulated PA reveals that the magnitude and phase of the output signal is affected by the supply voltage. Especially the gain dependency on the supply voltage brings disadvantages for a class-G system. In all systems developed in this work the magnitude of the gain is increased with increased supply voltage levels. This can be clearly seen in the AM/AM characteristics shown in Fig. 7.6. With DPD it is possible to restore the linearity to provide a flat system gain. Therefore, the predistorter also adjusts the envelope amplitude of the PA input signal. In the region of the supply voltage transition, the envelope amplitude is not unique anymore and one amplitude level corresponds to two output power levels, depending on the supply voltage. This has the disadvantage that the predistorter output signal is not usable to extract the class-G supply modulator input signal by using an envelope detector, which is a widespread practice for continuously supply modulated systems. In some applications it is required to replace a single-input single-output PA with a highly efficient solution. It is found that by applying synchronous gate bias modulation it is possible to remove the discontinuity which will allow extraction of the modulator control signal based on the envelope amplitude. This concept is published in [71] and presented in the following. For the evaluation of gate bias modulation, a modulator with a push-pull switching stage is attached to the gate bias of a RF PA, as shown in Fig. 7.9. In contrast to the class-G supply modulator switching stage, a push-pull configuration is chosen to ensure proper discharge of the gate bias node, since almost no gate current is consumed by the PA.

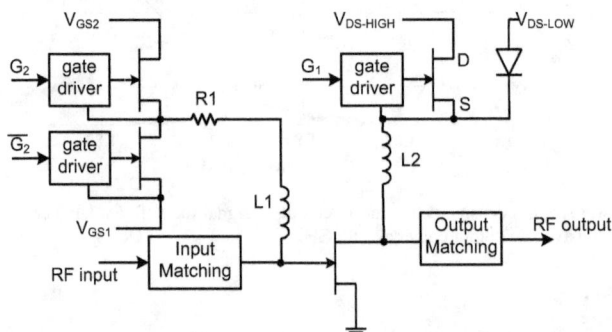

Fig. 7.9: Simplified schematic of the gate modulated class-G PA system. Common GND omitted for supplies, RF input and RF output signals.

The PA is operated with class-G supply modulation only and a fixed gate-source bias and with gate-modulation at a fixed V_{DS}. The AM/AM and AM/PM results are shown in Fig. 7.10. The gate bias modulation reduces the gate-source bias by 300 mV for signal powers below −5 dB normalized P_{IN}. The comparison of both plots reveals that a combination of gate bias and supply modulation will reduce either the AM/AM or the AM/PM discontinuity only, while the other discontinuity will be increased.

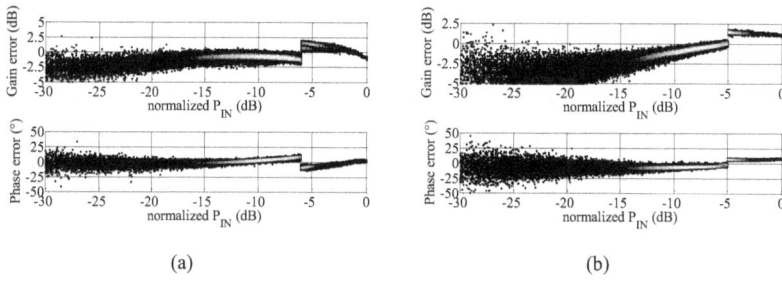

Fig. 7.10: AM/AM and AM/PM characteristics (a) for class-G supply modulation and (b) for gate bias modulation.

Thus, one concludes that gate-bias modulation is not usable to mitigate the linearity degradation caused by the class-G supply modulation, as intended, but provides other benefits. For the single-input single-output system, for instance, it is desirable to remove the AM/AM discontinuity only. The result for an AM/AM optimized gate bias setting is shown in Fig. 7.11 for the PA output (a) without DPD and (b) the PA input signal generated by the DPD processor. The marked area shows memory effects and amplitude compression that still contribute to errors if the modulator control signal is extracted from the envelope amplitude. This can be reduced by selecting a lower threshold for supply voltage switching at the cost of efficiency improvement.

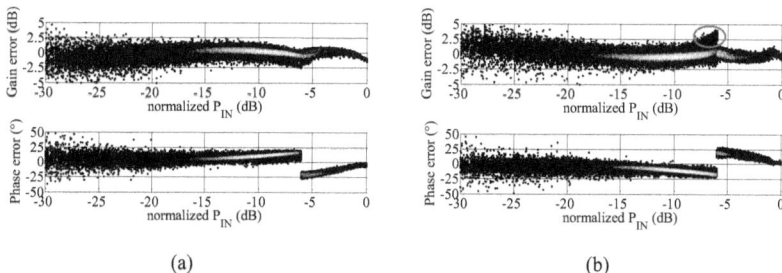

Fig. 7.11: AM/AM and AM/PM characteristics for a combined gate bias and class-G supply modulation (a) with optimized AM/AM characteristics and (b) the corresponding predistorted PA input signal.

7.2.4 79W three-level class-G systems with over 38% PAE at 1.8GHz and 120 MHz instantaneous modulation bandwidth

This system represents the latest development. It is designed to provide an IBW of 120 MHz, allowing the use of broadband carrier aggregated signals [44]. The system is based on the one presented in [72] with a modified drain bias network. The high modulation bandwidth is achieved by a new class-G supply modulator that can generate pulses with minimum pulse duration down to 2.5 ns. The modulator belongs to the third generation of modulators developed in this work (see 4.3.3).

Hardware design

The PA is based on a packaged FBH GaN-HEMT with a total gate width of 16 mm. For the PA design the high instantaneous modulation bandwidth in combination with the supply modulation requires a low impedance baseband termination in the drain-bias network with a high cut-off frequency to minimize linearity degradation [73]. The bandwidth of the baseband termination competes with the bandwidth of the RF-choke used for isolation in the RF domain. Therefore, a trade-off must be found, which in this design is achieved by a $\lambda/4$-wavelength stub with a characteristic impedance of 30 Ω, used as RF-choke. A photo of the PA and the class-G supply modulator is shown in Fig. 7.12 (a) and (b,c), respectively.

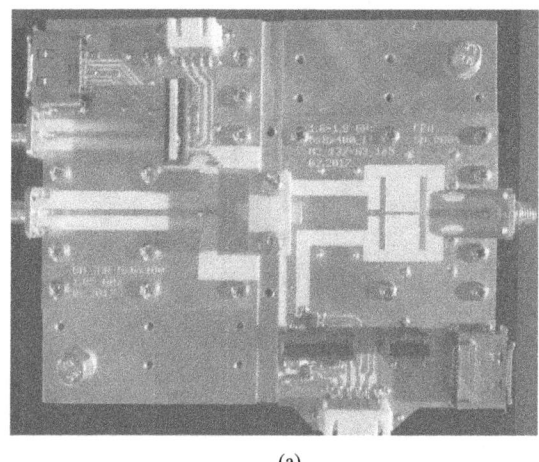

(a)

(b) (c)

Fig. 7.12: (a) Picture of the 79 W 1.8 GHz three-level class-G supply modulated PA and (b), (c) the class-G supply modulator.

Measurement results

The CW measurement results for different V_{DS} are shown in Fig. 7.13 for a frequency sweep at fixed output power levels, for (a) G_T and (b) PAE. As for the previously presented design, the supply voltage influences the matching and the operational band is shifted towards lower frequencies with reduced supply voltages. The PAE measurements show that the optimum PAE is outside the band, independently of the supply voltage level.

For the evaluation of the class-G system, a contiguous carrier-aggregated signal is used. It consists of 11 LTE-like carriers with IQ-modulation bandwidths in the range from 5 to 20 MHz each and an overall bandwidth of 120 MHz. The PAPR of the signal is 11.9 dB. The PSD and the amplitude CDF of the signal are plotted in Fig. 7.14 (a) and (b).

7 Class-G RF Power Amplifier System Optimization

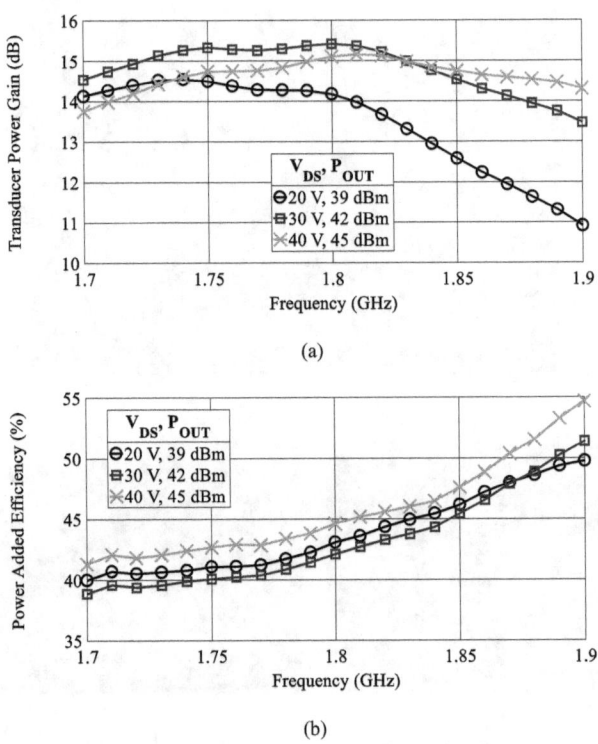

Fig. 7.13: CW frequency sweep measurements at different V_{DS} with fixed output power. (a) transducer power gain and (b) PAE.

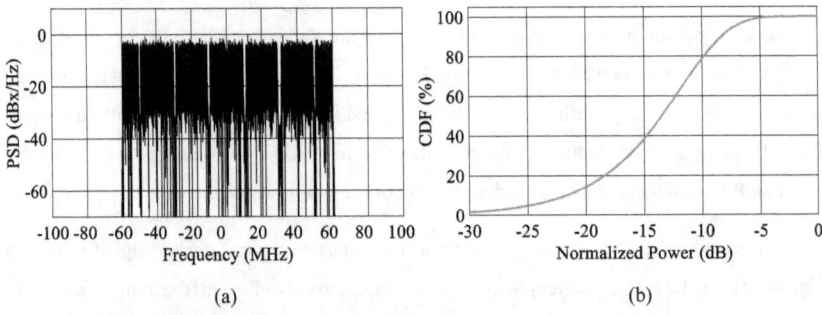

Fig. 7.14: (a) PSD and (b) amplitude CDF of the 120 MHz test signal.

The optimization of the three supply voltage levels yielded values of 18 V, 30 V, and 42 V. The supply switching thresholds are chosen to be 38.6 dBm and 41.6 dBm output power. Below the lowest threshold, the PA is supplied with 18 V. In between the thresholds the supply voltage is switched to 30 V and otherwise 42 V. The PA is biased in very deep class-AB with a quiescent current of 250 mA.

In dynamic operation an average output power of 39 dBm at 1.8 GHz is achieved while the ACLR is kept below −46 dB. The measured peak power is 49 dBm. The PAPR of the test signal is reduced to 10 dB by hard clipping, preserving the phase angle to prevent the DPD algorithm from overdriving the PA. The measured PSD for different average output power levels are presented in Fig. 7.15 (a). An extraction of the corresponding time domain envelope signal is shown in Fig. 7.15 (b).

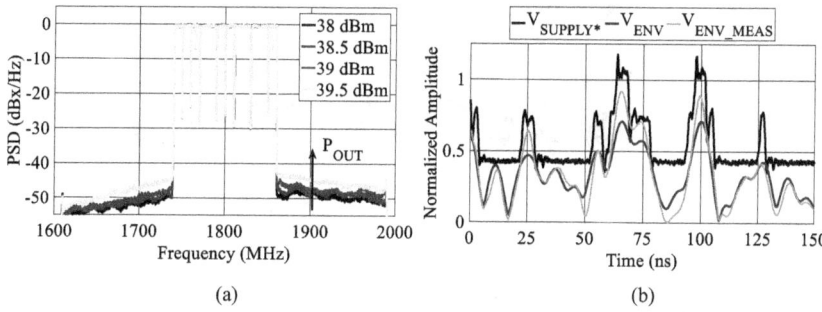

Fig. 7.15: (a) PSD for different output power levels and (b) time domain envelope signal and supply voltage. Supply voltage is measured at 50 Ω load impedance, since the class-G system does not provide a proper interface for measuring.

AM/AM and the AM/PM distortion are plotted in Fig. 7.16 (a) before and (b) after DPD linearization. Strong memory effects are visible without DPD, especially in the power back-off region where the PA is operated at the 18 V supply voltage. With DPD linearization, the linearity is restored and the memory effects are suppressed. At the supply voltage switching thresholds the distortions are not fully compensated by the linearization. This is assumed to be caused by the limited bandwidth of the DPD predistortion which is 380 MHz. The PAE of the full system reaches 38.5% which constitutes an increase of ~13 percentage-points compared to the operation with fixed supply voltage.

7 Class-G RF Power Amplifier System Optimization

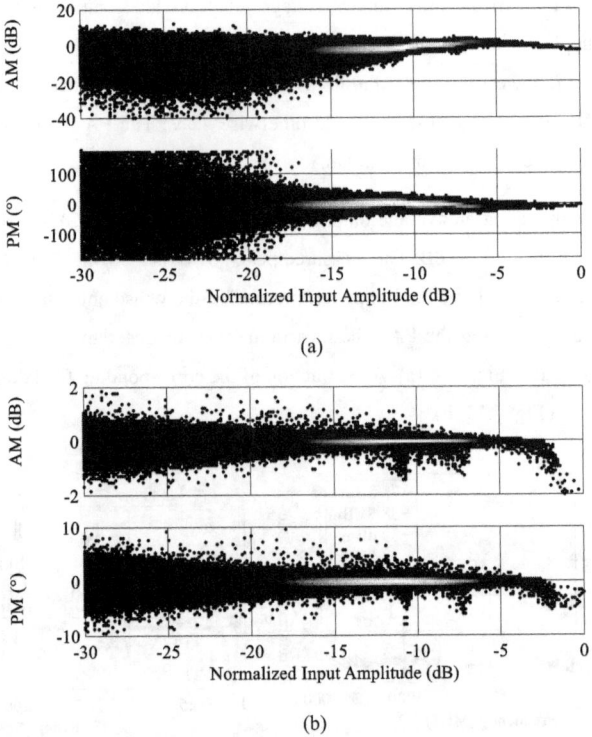

Fig. 7.16: AM/AM and AM/PM distortion (a) before and (b) after DPD linearization for operation with 39 dBm average output power at 1.8 GHz.

Summary

The instantaneous modulation bandwidth of 120 MHz and the high linearity in combination with DPD achieved with the above prototype represented a major progress for the class-G supply modulation topology. This performance allows full coverage of a state-of-the-art 100 MHz LTE advanced communication band and, therefore, makes the system a promising candidate for the future 5th generation of mobile communication networks, where carrier aggregation of 100 MHz carriers to a total bandwidth of up to 1 GHz are expected [74]. The limitations of the instantaneous modulation bandwidth IBW seen in the drain supply path could be circumvented by an increased RF frequency. Nevertheless, the increase of the supply switching frequency with the IBW will increase the switching losses in the class-G supply modulator and might be a limiting factor for efficiency enhancement.

8 Summary and Outlook

Class-G supply modulation of RF power amplifiers has shown to be an efficiency enhancement technique with promising capabilities. The suitability for state-of-the art modulation techniques with high peak-to-average power ratios for base station transmitter applications has been demonstrated successfully in this work.

First, the theory of ideal power amplifiers operated with supply modulation is derived. The properties of the GaN-HEMT devices are then analyzed and the deviation from the idealized power amplifier theory is discussed. The theoretical efficiency improvement for modulated signals with different signal properties is also analyzed. Furthermore, the linearity degradation caused by class-G supply modulation was investigated. The theoretical considerations are transferred to several prototype RF power amplifiers for optimized operation with class-G supply modulation with a carrier frequency in the 1.8 to 2.7 GHz range. It is shown that charge trapping effects in the GaN-HEMT devices cause deviations between theory and implementation and must be considered carefully for optimum operation.

As a key contribution of this work, GaN-based class-G supply modulators were developed. RF GaN technology is used to provide fast supply voltage switching. Since this limits the device types to normally-on n-type, the development of high-side gate drivers based on a floating architecture were designed and evaluated. High switching speed of the class-G supply modulator is important for efficiency improved operation with wideband modulated signals. The modulators developed provide switching speeds above 200 MHz and were used for instantaneous modulation bandwidths of up to 120 MHz.

The combination of RF power amplifier and class-G supply modulator results in a full efficiency-enhanced system. It is shown that an efficiency improvement between 10 to 18 percentage-points is achievable for systems with two or three supply voltage levels. For the characterization a measurement setup was built and optimized for the operation with the multiple-input single-output class-G system. The measurements revealed that the RF power amplifier characteristics change with the supply voltage which causes linearity degradation. To achieve competitive performance, digital predistortion linearization is applied. Due to the discretized supply voltage levels, the transfer characteristics of a class-G system exhibit discontinuities in gain and phase which cannot be corrected by most behavioral models. Accordingly, for improved linearization performance, a class-G optimized model was developed.

The class-G results achieved for wideband modulated signals, with an instantaneous modulation bandwidth beyond 100 MHz, open up a variety of applications in future mobile communications for this architecture. For the upcoming 5th generation of mobile communication systems, it will be a very attractive candidate that can compete against the established Doherty architecture. While Doherty power amplifiers only operate over a fixed output power back-off range, a class-G supply modulated power amplifier allows reconfiguration of the output power back-off range and can adapt to changes in the signal statistics. This will be an important feature in flexible carrier-aggregated systems, where the performance enhancement can be maintained if single carriers are switched on or off.

Moreover, the digital interfacing of the class-G supply modulator is a further step towards a digital transmitter and can be directly integrated into the baseband processor. Contrary to a continuously supply-modulated system, no envelope detector or additional analog input is required, and the modulated supply voltage can easily be synchronized with the RF signal in the software without the need for additional RF delay lines.

Further promising fields are space applications. In this field, solid-state power amplifiers are emerging and challenge the established travelling wave tube amplifiers. With an efficiency enhancement technique like class-G supply modulation, an alternative solution is available. For the presently used signals, the improvement might be limited due to the highly compressed signals with low output peak-to-average power ratio and the low requirements on linearity. However, this will change in the future, if modulation techniques with higher spectral efficiency are applied.

A performance limitation for the class-G solution is found in the gate driver circuitry of the modulator and the switching losses that scale with the instantaneous modulation bandwidth. The switch transistors used are based on RF GaN-HEMT technology and require a high-side gate driver. The presently used solutions result in considerable static power dissipation in the gate-driver, which makes the system inefficient for output powers in the milli-Watt range.

Overall, with this work conducted in the relative short time span of less than four years, class-G supply modulation of RF power amplifiers has emerged from a theoretical concept to the first choice architecture for wideband high-power operation within the various supply modulation techniques.

9 Appendix

9.1 Conduction angles, quiescent and ac current

The theory of a reduced drain-source current conduction angle is modified to simulate the behavior of the PA classes with continuous and discrete level supply modulation at output power back-off. The following calculations are used for the extraction of the DC current consumption and fundamental of the AC current as function of the quiescent and maximum drain-source current. Since this is independent of the drains-source voltage it is equivalent as for the reduced conduction angle theory [7]. The DC current is required to calculate the DC input power and the LF input impedance as function of the V_{DS}. In combination with the fundamental load impedance, the fundamental of the drain-source current is used to calculate the output voltage swing and the output power.

For the following calculations a period of the normalized drain-source current ($i_{DS}(\theta)$) as function of the angle θ ($-\pi < \theta <= \pi$) is defined: A constant level, representing the bias quiescent current (I_{DSQ}), is added to a cosine waveform with amplitude ($I_{MAX} - I_{DSQ} = g_m \cdot V_{GS\_AC1}$), which is dependent on the input excitation (V_{GS_AC1}), with negative current values clipped to zero. This is defined by (50) and (51) and shown in Fig. 9.1. The maximum current (I_{MAX}) defines the peak current and is defined in the range from zero to one, while I_{DSQ} can be defined in the range from $-\infty$ to 1.

$$\alpha = \begin{cases} 2 \cdot \pi & , \quad \frac{I_{DSQ}}{I_{MAX} - I_{DSQ}} > 1 \\ 2 \cdot \mathrm{acos}\left(\frac{I_{DSQ}}{I_{MAX} - I_{DSQ}}\right) & , \quad \text{otherwise} \\ 0 & , \quad \frac{I_{DSQ}}{I_{MAX} - I_{DSQ}} < -1 \end{cases} \quad (50)$$

$$i_{DS}(\theta) = \begin{cases} I_{DSQ} + (I_{MAX} - I_{DSQ}) \cdot \cos(\theta) & , \quad -\frac{\alpha}{2} < \theta < \frac{\alpha}{2} \\ 0 & , \quad \text{otherwise} \end{cases} \quad (51)$$

With the definition of the periodical drain-source current and the conduction angle the DC drain-source current (I_{DS_DC}) and the amplitude of the fundamental of the AC drain-source current ($\hat{i}_{DS\_AC1}$) can be calculated using a Fourier series as shown by (52) and (53). An overview of the relationship between I_{DS_DC} and $\hat{i}_{DS\_AC1}$ is shown in Fig. 9.2 for quiescent currents related to class-A to class-B. There it can be seen, that only the class-B condition

9 Appendix

($I_{DSQ} = 0$) provides a linear relationship between AC and DC current, while for all other settings the DC current reduction is limited by I_{DSQ}.

$$I_{DS\_DC} = \frac{1}{\pi} \cdot \left[I_{DSQ} \cdot \frac{\alpha}{2} + (I_{Max} - I_{DSQ}) \cdot \sin\left(\frac{\alpha}{2}\right) \right] \quad (52)$$

$$\hat{i}_{DS\_AC1} = \frac{2}{\pi} \cdot \left[I_{DSQ} \cdot \sin\left(\frac{\alpha}{2}\right) + \frac{(I_{Max} - I_{DSQ})}{2} \cdot \left(\frac{\alpha}{2} + \sin\left(\frac{\alpha}{2}\right) \cdot \cos\left(\frac{\alpha}{2}\right) \right) \right] \quad (53)$$

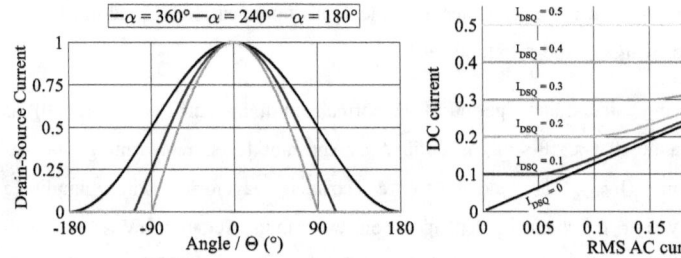

Fig. 9.1: Drain-source current waveforms for different quiescent currents and amplitudes.

Fig. 9.2: DC current for different quiescent drain-source currents (I_{DSQ}) vs. RMS AC current.

9.2 Intermodulation distortion

For the basic calculation of intermodulation distortion products located around the carrier frequency, the following formula based on a Taylor series is used to define the nonlinear distortion function:

$$\begin{aligned} y(t) &= \sum_{n=0}^{N} y_n(t) \\ &= \sum_{n=0}^{N} a_n \cdot (\text{Re}\{x_{BB}(t) \cdot e^{j \cdot 2 \cdot \pi \cdot f_0 \cdot t}\})^n \\ &= \sum_{n=0}^{N} a_n \cdot (I \cdot \cos(2\pi f_0 t) - Q \cdot \sin(2\pi f_0 t))^n \end{aligned} \quad (54)$$

Thereby I denotes the in-phase and Q the quadrature component of the complex baseband signal $\underline{x_{BB}}(t)$ which are modulated on the carrier frequency f_0. It is assumed that the bandwidth of I and Q is significantly smaller than f_0. Each element in the series defines the influence of

9 Appendix

the nonlinear order defined by n. The exponentiation of the signal causes the generation of new frequency components. To evaluate the distortions caused by a specific order n of the series (54) is evaluated separately for each n with $\omega_0 = 2\cdot\pi\cdot f_0$:

$$y_1(t) = I\cdot\cos(\omega_0\cdot t) - Q\cdot\sin(\omega_0\cdot t)] \quad (55)$$

The first order terms (55) only contain frequencies around ω_0. The higher order intermodulation products can be calculated iteratively based on (56):

$$y_n(t) = y_1(t)\cdot y_{n-1}(t) \quad (56)$$

With (57) and (58) the harmonics of the intermodulation products can be calculated for each frequency component. Thereby it is directly visible, that frequency components at the sum and difference of two single tones are generated when they are multiplied. Therefore, even order terms only generate even order harmonics and odd order terms generate odd order harmonics and must be considered for the linearization since they are located inside and close to the modulation band.

$$\sin(a)\cdot\sin(b) = \frac{1}{2}[\cos(a-b) - \cos(a+b)] \quad (57)$$

$$\sin(a)\cdot\cos(b) = \frac{1}{2}[\sin(a-b) + \sin(a+b)] \quad (58)$$

The second order term generates only harmonics located at DC and $2\cdot\omega_0$ as shown in (59):

$$y_2(t) = \frac{1}{2}\cdot[I^2 + Q^2 + \\ \cos(2\cdot\omega_0\cdot t)\cdot(I^2 - Q^2) + \\ \sin(2\cdot\omega_0\cdot t)\cdot(-2\cdot I\cdot Q)] \quad (59)$$

The third order terms can be calculated according to (56) by multiplication of (55) and (59) and odd order harmonics are generated (60). The frequency components of interest are located close to ω_0. Only frequency components around DC and $2\cdot\omega_0$ will result in intermodulation products around the carrier frequency if they are multiplied with ω_0:

9 Appendix

$$y_3(t) = \frac{1}{4} \cdot [\cos(\omega_0 \cdot t) \cdot (3 \cdot I^3 + 3 \cdot I \cdot Q^2) +$$

$$\sin(\omega_0 \cdot t) \cdot (-3 \cdot I^2 \cdot Q - 3 \cdot Q^3) +$$

$$\cos(3 \cdot \omega_0 \cdot t) \cdot (I^3 - 3 \cdot I^2 \cdot Q) +$$

$$\sin(3 \cdot \omega_0 \cdot t) \cdot (-3 \cdot I^2 \cdot Q + Q^3)]$$

(60)

The marked components cause distortions inside and around the modulated band and must be considered by the linearization algorithm. For higher order intermodulation products, the complexity increases rapidly.

10 Symbols and abbreviations

2DEG	two-dimensional electron gas
4G	4th generation of mobile networks
AC	alternating current
ACLR	adjacent channel leakage ratio
ADC	analog-to-digital converter
AM/AM	input amplitude dependent distortion of the output signal amplitude
AM/PM	input amplitude dependent distortion of the output signal phase
AVG	averaging factor
AWG	arbitrary waveform generator
b	relative bandwidth
B	bandwidth
BPSK	binary phase-shift keying
CCDF	complementary cumulative distribution function
CDF	cumulative distribution function
CW	continuous wave, continuous wave
DAC	digital-to-analog converter
DC	direct current
DPD	digital predistortion
DR	dynamic range
DSO	digital sampling scope
EER	envelope elimination and restoration
ENOB	effective number of bits
ET	envelope tracking
EVM	error vector magnitude
FBH	Ferdinand-Braun-Institut
FIR	finite impulse response
f_{MAX}	maximum oscillation frequency
$\underline{G}$	complex valued gain
GaAs	gallium arsenide
GaN	gallium-nitride, gallium nitride
g_m	transconductance
GMP	generalized memory polynomial
G_T	transducer power gain
IDFT	inverse discrete Fourier transformation
I_{DS_MAX}	maximum drain-source current
I_{DSQ}	quiescent drain-source current
ILA	iterative learning architecture
ILC	iterative learning control
IM	intermodulation
LF	low frequency
LTE	long term evolution
NMSE	normalized mean-square error
OFDM	orthogonal frequency-division-multiplexing
OVS	oversampling factor
PA	power amplifier
PAE	power-added efficiency
PAPR	peak-to-average power ratio
PCB	printed circuit board

PDF	probability distribution function
PH	parallel Hammerstein
P_{OUT}	output power
p_{PE}	piezoelectric polarization
p_{SP}	spontaneous polarization
P_{TH}	threshold power level
QAM	quadrature amplitude modulation
RF	radio frequency
R_L	load resistance
R_{L1}	fundamental load resistance
RMS	root mean square
R_{ON}	on-resistance
R_P	parallel resistor
R_S	series resistor
Si	silicon
SiC	silicon carbide
SNR	signal-to-noise ratio
SOA	safe operating area
$V_{DS\_AC\_REL}$	ratio between AC amplitude and DC drain-source supply voltage
VNA	vector network analyzer
α	drain current conduction angle

11 References

[1] W. Van Heddeghem, S. Lambert, B. Lannoo, D. Colle, M. Pickavet, P. Demeester, "Trends in worldwide ICT electricity consumption from 2007 to 2012," *Computer Communications*, vol. 50, pp. 64-76, Sep., 2014.

[2] Ericcson AB, "ERICSSON MOBILITY REPORT," Jun., 2017, Online, Accessed on Sep. 06, 2017.

[3] H.T. Friis, "A Note on a Simple Transmission Formula," *Proceedings of the IRE*, vol. 34, no. 5, pp. 254-256, May, 1946.

[4] O. Blume, D. Zeller, U. Barth, "Approaches to energy efficient wireless access networks," in *4th International Symposium on Communications, Control and Signal Processing*, Limassol, Cyprus, Mar., 2010, pp. 1-5.

[5] S. H. Han, J. H. Lee, "An overview of peak-to-average power ratio reduction techniques for multicarrier transmission," *IEEE Wireless Communications*, vol. 12, no, 2, pp. 56-65, Apr., 2005.

[6] E. Lawrey, C.J. Kikkert, "Peak to average power ratio reduction of OFDM signals using peak reduction carriers," in *Proceedings of the Fifth International Symposium on Signal Processing and Its Applications*, Brisbane, Australia, Aug., 1999, pp. 737-740.

[7] S. Cripps, RF Power Amplifiers for Wireless Communications, 2nd ed., Artech House, 2006.

[8] T. Sampei, S. Ohashi, "A new high efficiency circuit," *NIKKEI ELECTRONICS*, pp. 74-87, Jul., 1976.

[9] F. H. Raab, "Average Efficiency of Class-G Power Amplifiers," *IEEE Transactions on Consumer Electronics*, vol. CE-32, no. 2, pp. 145-150, May, 1986.

[10] C. Buoli, A. Abbiati, D. Riccardi, "Microwave power amplifier with "envelope controlled" drain power supply," in *European Microwave Conference*, Bologna, Italy, Sep., 1995, pp. 31-35.

[11] N. Wolff, W. Heinrich, O. Bengtsson, "Challenges in the design of wideband GaN-HEMT based class-G RF-power amplifiers," in *German Microwave Conference*, Bochum, Germany, May, 2016, pp. 189-192.

11 References

[12] José C. Pedro, Luís C. Nunes, Pedro M. Cabral, "Soft compression and the origins of nonlinear behavior of GaN HEMTs," in *European Microwave Conference*, Rome, Italy, Oct., 2014, pp. 1297-1300.

[13] N. Ramanan, B. Lee, V. Misra, "Device Modeling for Understanding AlGaN/GaN HEMT Gate-Lag," *IEEE Transactions on Electron Devices*, vol. 61, no. 6, pp. 2012-2018, Jun., 2014.

[14] G. Meneghesso, G. Verzellesi, R. Pierobon, F. Rampazzo, A. Chini, U. K. Mishra, C. Canali, E. Zanoni, "Surface-related drain current dispersion effects in AlGaN-GaN HEMTs," *IEEE Transactions on Electron Devices*, vol. 51, no. 10, pp. 1554-1561, Oct., 2004.

[15] U. K. Mishra, L. Shen, T. E. Kazior, Y. Wu, "GaN-Based RF Power Devices and Amplifiers," *Proceedings of the IEEE*, vol. 96, no. 2, pp. 287-305, Jan., 2008.

[16] L. F. Eastman et al., "Undoped AlGaN/GaN HEMTs for microwave power amplification," *IEEE Transactions on Electron Devices*, vol. 48, no. 3, pp. 479-485, Mar., 2001.

[17] K. R. Bagnall, O. I. Saadat, S. Joglekar, T. Palacios, E. N. Wang, "Experimental Characterization of the Thermal Time Constants of GaN HEMTs Via Micro-Raman Thermometry," *IEEE Trans. Electron. Devices*, vol. 64, no. 5, pp. 2121-2128, May., 2017.

[18] Earl McCune, "Operating modes of dynamic-power-supply transmitter amplifiers," *IEEE Transactions on Microwave Theory and Techniques*, vol. 62, no. 11, pp. 2511-2517, Nov., 2014.

[19] I. Angelov, H. Zirath, N. Rosman, "A new empirical nonlinear model for HEMT and MESFET devices," *IEEE Transactions on Microwave Theory and Techniques*, vol. 40, no.12, pp. 2258-2266, Dec., 1992.

[20] M. Olavsbråten, D. Gecan, M. R. Duffy, G. Lasser, Z. Popovic, "Efficiency enhancement and linearization of GaN PAs using reduced-bandwidth supply modulation," in *European Microwave Conference*, Nuremberg, Germany, Oct., 2017, pp.456-459.

[21] A. Alt, J. Lees, "Improving efficiency, linearity and linearisability of an asymmetric doherty power amplifier by modulating the peaking Amplifier's supply voltage," in *European Microwave Conference*, Nuremberg, Germany, Oct., 2017, pp. 464-467.

11 References

[22] D. Čučak et al., "Physics-Based Analytical Model for Input, Output, and Reverse Capacitance of a GaN HEMT With the Field-Plate Structure," *IEEE Transactions on Power Electronics*, vol. 32, no. 3, pp. 2189-2202, Mar., 2017.

[23] 3GPP TS 36.104 V13.6.0 Release 13, 2017.

[24] Detailed specifications of the terrestrial radio interfaces of International Mobile Telecommunications Advanced (IMT-Advanced), Recommendation ITU-R M.2012-1(02/2014), pp. 1-138, 2014.

[25] E. McCune, "Dynamic Power Supply Transmitters," Cambridge University Press, 2015.

[26] P. Asbeck, Z. Popovic, "ET Comes of Age: Envelope Tracking for Higher-Efficiency Power Amplifiers," *IEEE Microwave Magazine*, vol. 17, no. 3, pp. 16-25, Mar., 2016.

[27] N. Wolff, W. Heinrich, O. Bengtsson, "The Efficiency/Bandwidth Trade-Off in Class-G Supply-Modulated Power Amplifiers," in *European Microwave Conference*, Nuremberg, Germany, Oct., 2017, pp. 472-475.

[28] N. Wolff, W. Heinrich, O. Bengtsson, "100-MHz GaN-HEMT Class-G Supply Modulator for High-Power Envelope-Tracking Applications," *IEEE Transactions on Microwave Theory and Techniques*, vol. 65, no. 3, pp. 872–880, Mar., 2017.

[29] M. R. Hontz, Y. Cao, M. C., R. Li, A. Garrido, R. Chu, R. Khanna, "Modeling and Characterization of Vertical GaN Schottky Diodes With AlGaN Cap Layers," *IEEE Transactions on Electron Devices*, vol. 64, no. 5, pp. 2172-2178, May., 2017.

[30] F. M. Barradas, L. C. Nunes, T. R. Cunha, P. M. Lavrador, P. M. Cabral, J. C. Pedro, "Compensation of Long-Term Memory Effects on GaN HEMT-Based Power Amplifiers," *IEEE Transactions on Microwave Theory and Techniques*, vol. 65, no. 9, pp. 3379-3388, Mar., 2017.

[31] R. Vetury, N.Q. Zhang, S. Keller, U.K. Mishra, "The impact of surface states on the DC and RF characteristics of AlGaN/GaN HFETs," *IEEE Transactions on Electron Devices*, vol. 48, no. 3, pp. 560-566, Mar., 2001.

[32] O. Jardel et al., "An Electrothermal Model for AlGaN/GaN Power HEMTs Including Trapping Effects to Improve Large-Signal Simulation Results on High VSWR,"

IEEE Transactions on Microwave Theory and Techniques, vol. 55, no. 12, pp. 2660-2669, Dec., 2007.

[33]   A. Benvegnù et al. "Characterization of Defects in AlGaN/GaN HEMTs Based on Nonlinear Microwave Current Transient Spectroscopy," *IEEE Transactions on Electron Devices*, vol. 64, no. 5, pp. 2135-2141, May, 2017.

[34]   C. Florian et al., "A Prepulsing Technique for the Characterization of GaN Power Amplifiers With Dynamic Supply Under Controlled Thermal and Trapping States," *IEEE Transactions on Microwave Theory and Techniques*, vol. 65, no. 12, pp. 5056-5062, Dec., 2017.

[35]   N. Wolff, T. Hoffmann, W. Heinrich, O. Bengtsson, "Impact of Drain-Lag Induced Current Degradation for a Dynamically Operated GaN-HEMT Power Amplifier," submitted to *IEEE MTT-S Int. Microwave Symposium*, Philadelphia, USA, Jun., 2018.

[36]   O. Bengtsson, S. A. Chevtchenko, R. Doerner, P. Kurpas, and W. Heinrich, "Load-Pull Investigation of a High-Voltage RF-Power GaN-HEMT Technology in Supply Modulated Applications ," *Frequenz*, vol. 65, no. 7-8, pp. 217-224, Aug., 2011.

[37]   O. Bengtsson, N. Wolff, S. A. Chevtchenko, J. Würfl, W. Heinrich, "Optimization of RF Power GaN-HEMTs for Class-G Operation in Supply-Modulated Systems," in *micro- and millimeter wave technology and techniques workshop*, esa-estec, 2014.

[38]   J. Rollet, "Stability and Power-Gain Invariants of Linear Twoports," *IRE Transactions on Circuit Theory*, vol. 9, no. 1, pp. 29-32, Mar., 1962.

[39]   G. Gonzalez, Microwave Transistor Amplifiers: Analysis and Design, 2nd ed.: Prentice Hall, 1996.

[40]   M. Krellmann, O. Bengtsson, W. Heinrich, "GaN-HEMTs as switches for high-power wideband supply modulators," in *European Microwave Conference*, Nuremberg, Germany, Oct., 2013, pp. 553-556.

[41]   Silicon Laboratories Inc., "Si861x/2x Data Sheet," Rev. 1.7, Datasheet, Accessed on Aug. 29, 2017.

[42]   Analog Devices Inc. "5 kV RMS/3.75 kV RMS, 600 Mbps, Dual-Channel LVDS Isolators," Rev. D, Datasheet, 2017, Accessed on Aug. 29, 2017.

11 References

[43] N. Wolff, O. Bengtsson., M. Schmidt, M. Berroth, W. Heinrich, "Linearity Analysis of a 40 W Class-G-Modulated Microwave Power Amplifier," in *European Microwave Conference*, Paris, France, Sep., 2015, pp. 1216-1219.

[44] N. Wolff, W. Heinrich, O.Bengtsson, "Highly Efficient 1.8 GHz Amplifier with 120 MHz Class-G Supply-Modulation," *IEEE Transactions on Microwave Theory and Techniques*, vol. 65, no. 12, pp. 5223-5230, Dec., 2017.

[45] N. Wolff, W. Heinrich, O. Bengtsson, "Benchmarking of RF Measurement Systems for Digital Predistortion using Iterative Learning Control," in *European Microwave Conference*, Nuremberg, Germany, Oct., 2017, pp. 668-671.

[46] IEEE Standard for Air Interface for Broadband Wireless Access Systems, IEEE Standard 802.16-2012 (Revision of IEEE Std 802.16-2009), p. 886, Aug., 2012.

[47] R. O'Neill, L. B. Lopes, "Envelope variations and spectral splatter in clipped multicarrier signals," in *Proceedings of 6th International Symposium on Personal, Indoor and Mobile Radio Communications*, Toronto, Canada, Sep., 1995, pp. 71-75.

[48] J. Armstrong, "Peak-to-average power reduction for OFDM by repeated clipping and frequency domain filtering," *Electronic Letters*, vol. 38, no. 5, pp. 246-247, Aug., 2002.

[49] A. Hyo-Sung, C. Yang Quan, and K. L. Moore, "Iterative Learning Control: Brief Survey and Categorization," *IEEE Transactions on Systems, Man, and Cybernetics, Part C*, vol. 37, pp. 1099-1121, Oct., 2007.

[50] J. Chani-Cahuana, P.N. Landing, C. Fager, T. Eriksson, "Structured Digital Predistorter Model Derivation Based on Iterative Learning Control," in *European Microwave Conference*, London, UK, Oct., 2016, pp. 178-181.

[51] J. Chani-Cahuan, P. N. Landin, C. Fager, T. Eriksson, "Iterative Learning Control for RF Power Amplifier Linearization," *IEEE Transactions on Microwave Theory and Techniques*, vol. 64, no. 9, pp. 2778-2789, Sep., 2016.

[52] P. Landin, Digital Baseband Modeling and Correction of Radio Frequency Power Amplifiers, 2012.

[53] D.R. Morgan, Z. Ma, J. Kim, M.G. Zierdt, J. Pastalan, "A Generalized Memory Polynomial Model for Digital Predistortion of RF Power Amplifiers," *IEEE Transactions on Signal Processing*, vol. 54, no. 10, pp. 3852-3860, Oct., 2006.

11 References

[54] S. Afsardoost, T. Eriksson, C. Fager, "Digital Predistortion Using a Vector-Switched Model," *IEEE Transactions on Microwave Theory and Techniques*, vol. 60, no. 4, pp. 1166-1174, Apr., 2012.

[55] N. Wolff, W. Heinrich, O. Bengtsson, "A Novel Model for Digital Predistortion of Discrete Level Supply-Modulated RF Power Amplifiers," *IEEE Microwave and Wireless Components Letters*, vol. 26, no. 2, pp. 146-148, Feb., 2016.

[56] P. Zhan, K. Qin, and S. Cai, "Joint compensation model for memory power amplifier and frequency-dependent nonlinear IQ impairments," *Electronic Letters*, vol. 47, no. 25, pp. 1382-1384, Dec. 2011.

[57] O. Hammi, A. Kwan, S. Bensmida, K. A. Morris, F. M. Ghannouchi, "A Digital Predistortion System With Extended Correction Bandwidth With Application to LTE-A Nonlinear Power Amplifiers," *IEEE Transactions on Circuits and Systems I: Regular Papers*, vol. 61, no. 12, pp. 3487-3495, Dec., 2014.

[58] T. Gotthans, R. Maršálek, J. Gotthans, "Wideband digital predistortion with sub-Nyquist nonuniform sampling and reconstruction of feedback path," in *IEEE Topical Conference on RF/Microwave Power Amplifiers for Radio and Wireless Applications*, Phoenix, USA, Jan., 2017, pp. 70-72.

[59] G. Watkins, J. Zhou, K. Morris, ">41% efficient 10W envelope modulated LTE downlink power amplifier," in *European Microwave Integrated Circuits Conference*, Manchester, UK, Oct., 2011, pp. 260-263.

[60] S. Yoo et al., "A class-G dual-supply switched-capacitor power amplifier in 65nm CMOS," in *Radio Frequency Integrated Circuits Symposium*, Montreal, Canada, Jun., 2012, pp 233-236.

[61] S. Yoo et al., "A Class-G Switched-Capacitor RF Power Amplifier," *IEEE Journal of Solid-State Circuits*, vol. 48, no. 5, pp. 1212-1224, May., 2013.

[62] A. Bräckle, L. Rathgeber, F. Siegert, S. Heck, M. Berroth, "Power supply modulation for RF applications," in *Power Electronics and Motion Control Conference*, Novi Sad, Serbia, Sep., 2012, pp. LS8d.3-1-LS8d.3-5.

[63] T. Fujiwara et al., "All Gallium Nitride Envelope-Tracking Multiband Power Amplifier Using 200MHz Switching Buck-Converter," in *European Microwave Integrated Circuits Conference*, London, UK, Oct., 2016, pp. 125-128.

11 References

[64] D. F. Kimball, H. Kazeimi, J. J. Yan, P. T. Theilmann, I. Telleiz, G. Collins, "Envelope Modulator & X-band MMICs On Highly Integrated 3D Tunable Microcoax Substrate," in *Compound Semiconductor Integrated Circuit Symposium*, New Orleans, USA, Oct., 2015, pp. 1-4.

[65] S. Sakata et al., "An 80MHz Modulation Bandwidth High Efficiency Multi-band Envelope-Tracking Power Amplifier Using GaN Single-Phase Buck-Converter," in *IEEE MTT-S International Microwave Symposium*, Honolulu, HI, Jun., 2017, pp. 1854-1857.

[66] P. T. Theilmann et al., "A 60MHz Bandwidth High Efficiency X-Band Envelope Tracking Power Amplifier," in *Compound Semiconductor Integrated Circuit Symposium*, Monterey, USA, Oct., 2013, pp. 1-4.

[67] M. Özen, C. Fager, "Symmetrical doherty amplifier with high efficiency over large output power dynamic range," in *IEEE MTT-S International Microwave Symposium*, Tampa, USA, Jun., 2014, pp. 1-4.

[68] M. N. A. Abadi, H. Golestaneh, H. Sarbishaei, S. Boumaiza, "Doherty Power Amplifier With Extended Bandwidth and Improved Linearizability Under Carrier-Aggregated Signal Stimuli," *IEEE Microwave Components Letters*, vol. 26, no. 5, pp. 358-360, May., 2016.

[69] S. Min, H. Christange, M. Szymanowski, "Two-Stage Integrated Doherty Power Amplifier with Extended Instantaneous Bandwidth for 4/5G Wireless Systems," in *IEEE MTT-S International Microwave Symposium*, Honolulu, USA, Jun., 2017, pp. 122-125.

[70] N. Wolff, W. Heinrich, O. Bengtsson, "A Three-Level Class-G Modulated 1.85 GHz RF Power Amplifier for LTE Applications with over 50% PAE," in *IEEE MTT-S International Microwave Symposium*, San Francisco, USA, 2016, pp. 1-4.

[71] N. Wolff, W. Heinrich, O. Bengtsson, "Discrete Gate Bias Modulation of a Class-G Modulated RF Power Amplifier," in *European Microwave Conference*, London, UK, Oct., 2016, pp. 827-830.

[72] N. Wolff, W. Heinrich, O. Bengtsson, "Highly Efficient Class-G Supply-Modulated Amplifier with 75 MHz Modulation Bandwidth for 1.8-1.9 GHz LTE FDD Applications," in *International Microwave Symposium*, Honolulu, USA, Jun., 2017, pp. 1842-1845.

11 References

[73] M. Akmal et al., "The effect of baseband impedance termination on the linearity of GaN HEMTs," in *European Microwave Conference*, Paris, France, Sep., 2010, pp. 1046-1049.

[74] K. Sundhar, L. C. Miller, 5G RF For Dummies®, John Wiley & Sons Inc., 2017.

12 Publications

[I] O. Bengtsson, **N. Wolff**, S.A. Chevtchenko, J. Würfl, and W. Heinrich, "Optimization of RF Power GaN-HEMTs for Class-G Operation in Supply-Modulated Systems," in *ESA Micro- and Millimetre Wave Technology and Techniques Workshop*, Nordwijk, The Netherlands, Nov., 2014.

[II] **N. Wolff**, W. Heinrich, and O. Bengtsson, "Analysis of the Switching Threshold in Dual-Level Class-G Modulated Power Amplifiers," in *Integrated Nonlinear Microwave and Millimetre-wave Circuits Workshop*, Taormina, Italy, Oct., 2015, pp. 1-3.

[III] S. Preis, A. Wiens, **N. Wolff**, R. Jakoby, W. Heinrich, O. Bengtsson, "Frequency-Agile Packaged GaN-HEMT using MIM Thickfilm BST Varactors," in *European Microwave Conference*, Paris, France, Sep., 2015, pp. 1291-1294.

[IV] **N. Wolff**, O. Bengtsson, M. Schmidt, M. Berroth, W. Heinrich, "Linearity Analysis of a 40 W Class-G-Modulated Microwave Power Amplifier," in *European Microwave Conference*, Paris, France, Sep., 2015, pp. 1216-1219.

[V] **N. Wolff**, O. Bengtsson, and W. Heinrich, "Complexity of DPD Linearization in the full RF-Band for a WiMAX Power Amplifier," in *German Microwave Conference*, Nuremberg, Germany, Mar., 2015, pp. 13-16.

[VI] O. Bengtsson, **N. Wolff**, S. Paul, T. Kuremyr, M. Krellmann, C. Delepaut, N. Ayllon, and W. Heinrich, "GaN in fast DC/DC converters for envelope tracking applications in space," in *8th Wide Bandgap Semiconductor and Components Workshop*, Harwell, UK, Sep., 2016.

[VII] **N. Wolff**, W. Heinrich and O. Bengtsson, "Discrete Gate Bias Modulation of a Class-G Modulated RF Power Amplifier," in *European Microwave Conference*, London, UK, Oct., 2016, pp. 827-830.

[VIII] S. Preis, J. Ferretti, **N. Wolff**, A. Wiens, R. Jakoby, W. Heinrich, O. Bengtsson, "Response Time of VSWR Protection for GaN HEMT based Power Amplifiers," in *European Microwave Conference*, London, UK, Oct., 2016, pp. 401-404.

[IX] **N. Wolff**, W. Heinrich, M. Berroth and O. Bengtsson, "A Three-Level Class-G Modulated 1.85 GHz RF Power Amplifier for LTE Applications with over 50% PAE," in *IEEE MTT-S International Microwave Symposium*, San Francisco, USA, May, 2016, pp. 1-4.

[X] **N. Wolff**, W. Heinrich, and O. Bengtsson, "Challenges in the Design of Wideband GaN-HEMT based Class-G RF-Power Amplifiers," in *German Microwave Conference*, Bochum, Germany, Mar., 2016, pp. 189-192.

[XI] S. Kelz, M. Schmidt, **N. Wolff**, M. Berroth, W. Heinrich, O. Bengtsson, "A 56 W Power Amplifier with 2-Level Supply and Load Modulation," in *German Microwave Conference*, Bochum, Germany, Mar., 2016, pp. 185-188.

[XII]   N. **Wolff**, W. Heinrich, and O. Bengtsson, "A Novel Model for Digital Predistortion of Discrete Level Supply-Modulated RF Power Amplifiers," *IEEE Microwave and Wireless Components Letters*, vol. 26, no. 2, pp. 146-148, Feb., 2016.

[XIII] **N. Wolff**, W. Heinrich, and O. Bengtsson, "100-MHz GaN-HEMT Class-G Supply Modulator for High-Power Envelope-Tracking Applications," *IEEE Transactions on Microwave Theory and Techniques*, vol. 65, no. 3, pp. 872-880, Mar., 2017.

[XIV] **N. Wolff**, W. Heinrich and O. Bengtsson, "Highly Efficient Class-G Supply-Modulated Amplifier with 75 MHz Modulation Bandwidth for 1.8-1.9 GHz LTE FDD Applications," in *IEEE MTT-S International Microwave Symposium*, Honolulu, USA, Jun., 2017, pp. 1842-1845.

[XV]   S. Preis, D. Kienemund, **N. Wolff**, H. Maune, R. Jakoby, W. Heinrich, O. Bengtsson, "Thick-Film MIM BST Varactors for GaN Power Amplifiers with Discrete Dynamic Load Modulation," in *IEEE MTT-S International Microwave Symposium*, Honolulu, USA, Jun., 2017, pp. 281-284.

[XVI] S. Paul, **N. Wolff**, C. Delepaut, V. Valenta, W. Heinrich, O. Bengtsson, "A 14 W Wideband Supply-Modulated System with Reverse Buck Converter and Floating-Ground RF Power Amplifier," in *IEEE MTT-S International Microwave Symposium*, Honolulu, USA, Jun., 2017, pp. 936-939.

[XVII] **N. Wolff**, W. Heinrich, O. Bengtsson, "Benchmarking of RF Measurement Systems for Digital Predistortion using Iterative Learning Control," in *European Microwave Conference*, Nuremberg, Oct., 2017, pp. 668-671.

[XVIII] **N. Wolff**, W. Heinrich, O. Bengtsson, "The Efficiency/Bandwidth Trade-Off in Class-G Supply-Modulated Power Amplifiers," in *European Microwave Conference*, Nuremberg, Germany, Oct., 2017, pp. 472-475.

[XIX] S. Paul, **N. Wolff**, C. Delepaut, V. Valenta, W. Heinrich, O. Bengtsson, "Pulsed RF Characterization of Envelope Tracking Systems for Improved Shaping Function Extraction," in *European Microwave Conference*, Nuremberg, Germany, Oct., 2017, pp. 664-667.

[XX]   **N. Wolff**, W. Heinrich, O. Bengtsson, "Highly Efficient 1.8 GHz Amplifier with 120 MHz Class-G Supply-Modulation," *IEEE Transactions on Microwave Theory and Techniques*, vol. 65, no. 12, Dec., 2017.

[XXI] S. Preis, **N. Wolff**, F. Lenze, A. Wiens, R. Jakoby, W. Heinrich, O. Bengtsson, "Load tuning assisted discrete-level supply modulation using BST and GaN devices for highly efficient power amplifiers," accepted for publication at *IEEE MTT-S International Microwave Symposium*, Philadelphia, USA, Jun., 2018.

[XXII] **N. Wolff**, T. Hoffmann, W. Heinrich, O. Bengtsson, "Impact of Drain-Lag Induced Current Degradation for a Dynamically Operated GaN-HEMT Power Amplifier," accepted for publication at *IEEE MTT-S International Microwave Symposium*, Philadelphia, USA, Jun., 2018.

[XXIII] **N. Wolff**, W. Heinrich, O. Bengtsson, "Class-G Supply Modulation for MIMO and Radar with Phased Array Antennas," submitted to *European Microwave Conference*, Madrid, Spain, Sep., 2018.

[XXIV] **N. Wolff**, W. Heinrich, O. Bengtsson, "Dynamic Over-Voltage Operation of a Discrete-Level Supply-Modulated GaN-based RF PA," submitted to *European Microwave Conference*, Madrid, Spain, Sep., 2018.

Innovationen mit Mikrowellen und Licht
Forschungsberichte aus dem Ferdinand-Braun-Institut,
Leibniz-Institut für Höchstfrequenztechnik

Herausgeber: Prof. Dr. G. Tränkle, Prof. Dr.-Ing. W. Heinrich

Band 1: **Thorsten Tischler**
Die Perfectly-Matched-Layer-Randbedingung in der
Finite-Differenzen-Methode im Frequenzbereich:
Implementierung und Einsatzbereiche
ISBN: 3-86537-113-2, 19,00 EUR, 144 Seiten

Band 2: **Friedrich Lenk**
Monolithische GaAs FET- und HBT-Oszillatoren
mit verbesserter Transistormodellierung
ISBN: 3-86537-107-8, 19,00 EUR, 140 Seiten

Band 3: **R. Doerner, M. Rudolph (eds.)**
Selected Topics on Microwave Measurements,
Noise in Devices and Circuits, and Transistor Modeling
ISBN: 3-86537-328-3, 19,00 EUR, 130 Seiten

Band 4: **Matthias Schott**
Methoden zur Phasenrauschverbesserung von
monolithischen Millimeterwellen-Oszillatoren
ISBN: 978-3-86727-774-0, 19,00 EUR, 134 Seiten

Band 5: **Katrin Paschke**
Hochleistungsdiodenlaser hoher spektraler Strahldichte
mit geneigtem Bragg-Gitter als Modenfilter (α-DFB-Laser)
ISBN: 978-3-86727-775-7, 19,00 EUR, 128 Seiten

Band 6: **Andre Maaßdorf**
Entwicklung von GaAs-basierten Heterostruktur-Bipolartransistoren
(HBTs) für Mikrowellenleistungszellen
ISBN: 978-3-86727-743-3, 23,00 EUR, 154 Seiten

Band 7: **Prodyut Kumar Talukder**
Finite-Difference-Frequency-Domain Simulation of Electrically
Large Microwave Structures using PML and Internal Ports
ISBN: 978-3-86955-067-1, 19,00 EUR, 138 Seiten

Band 8: **Ibrahim Khalil**
Intermodulation Distortion in GaN HEMT
ISBN: 978-3-86955-188-3, 23,00 EUR, 158 Seiten

Band 9: **Martin Maiwald**
Halbleiterlaser basierte Mikrosystemlichtquellen für die Raman-Spektroskopie
ISBN: 978-3-86955-184-5, 19,00 EUR, 134 Seiten

Band 10: **Jens Flucke**
Mikrowellen-Schaltverstärker in GaN- und GaAs-Technologie
Designgrundlagen und Komponenten
ISBN: 978-3-86955-304-7, 21,00 EUR, 122 Seiten

Cuvillier Verlag
Internationaler wissenschaftlicher Fachverlag

Innovationen mit Mikrowellen und Licht
Forschungsberichte aus dem Ferdinand-Braun-Institut, Leibniz-Institut für Höchstfrequenztechnik

Herausgeber: Prof. Dr. G. Tränkle, Prof. Dr.-Ing. W. Heinrich

Band 11: Harald Klockenhoff
Optimiertes Design von Mikrowellen-Leistungstransistoren und Verstärkern im X-Band
ISBN: 978-3-86955-391-7, 26,75 EUR, 130 Seiten

Band 12: Reza Pazirandeh
Monolithische GaAs FET- und HBT-Oszillatoren mit verbesserter Transistormodellierung
ISBN: 978-3-86955-107-8, 19,00 EUR, 140 Seiten

Band 13: Tomas Krämer
High-Speed InP Heterojunction Bipolar Transistors and Integrated Circuits in Transferred Substrate Technology
ISBN: 978-3-86955-393-1, 21,70 EUR, 140 Seiten

Band 14: Phuong Thanh Nguyen
Investigation of spectral characteristics of solitary diode lasers with integrated grating resonator
ISBN: 978-3-86955-651-2, 24,00 EUR, 156 Seiten

Band 15: Sina Riecke
Flexible Generation of Picosecond Laser Pulses in the Infrared and Green Spectral Range by Gain-Switching of Semiconductor Lasers
ISBN: 978-3-86955-652-9, 22,60 EUR, 136 Seiten

Band 16: Christian Hennig
Hydrid-Gasphasenepitaxie von versetzungsarmen und freistehenden GaN-Schichten
ISBN: 978-3-86955-822-6, 27,00 EUR, 162 Seiten

Band 17: Tim Wernicke
Wachstum von nicht- und semipolaren InAlGaN-Heterostrukturen für hocheffiziente Licht-Emitter
ISBN: 978-3-86955-881-3, 23,40 EUR, 138 Seiten

Band 18: Andreas Wentzel
Klasse-S Mikrowellen-Leistungsverstärker mit GaN-Transistoren
ISBN: 978-3-86955-897-4, 29,65 EUR, 172 Seiten

Band 19: Veit Hoffmann
MOVPE growth and characterization of (In,Ga)N quantum structures for laser diodes emitting at 440 nm
ISBN: 978-3-86955-989-6, 18,00 EUR, 118 Seiten

Band 20: Ahmad Ibrahim Bawamia
Improvement of the beam quality of high-power broad area semiconductor diode lasers by means of an external resonator
ISBN: 978-3-95404-065-0, 21,00 EUR, 126 Seiten

Cuvillier Verlag
Internationaler wissenschaftlicher Fachverlag

Innovationen mit Mikrowellen und Licht
Forschungsberichte aus dem Ferdinand-Braun-Institut, Leibniz-Institut für Höchstfrequenztechnik

Herausgeber: Prof. Dr. G. Tränkle, Prof. Dr.-Ing. W. Heinrich

Band 21: **Agnietzka Pietrzak**
Realization of High Power Diode Lasers with Extremely Narrow Vertical Divergence
ISBN: 978-3-95404-066-7, 27,40 EUR, 144 Seiten

Band 22: **Eldad Bahat-Treidel**
GaN-based HEMTs for High Voltage Operation
Design, Technology and Characterization
ISBN: 978-3-95404-094-0, 41,10 EUR, 220 Seiten

Band 23: **Ponky Ivo**
AlGaN/GaN HEMTs Reliability:
Degradation Modes and Anslysis
ISBN: 978-3-95404-259-3, 23,55 EUR, 132 Seiten

Band 24: **Stefan Spießberger**
Compact Semiconductor-Based Laser Sources
with Narrow Linewidth and High Output Power
ISBN: 978-3-95404-261-6, 24,15 EUR, 140 Seiten

Band 25: **Silvio Kühn**
Mikrowellenoszillatoren für die Erzeugung von atmosphärischen Mikroplasmen
ISBN: 978-3-95404-378-1, 21,85 EUR, 112 Seiten

Band 26: **Sven Schwertfeger**
Experimentelle Untersuchung der Modensynchronisation in Multisegment-Laserdioden zur Erzeugung kurzer optischer Pulse bei einer Wellenlänge von 920 nm
ISBN: 978-3-95404-471-9, 29,45 EUR, 150 Seiten

Band 27: **Christoph Matthias Schultz**
Analysis and mitigation of the factors limiting the effiency of high power distributed feedback diode lasers
ISBN: 978-3-95404-521-1, 68,40 EUR, 388 Seiten

Band 28: **Luca Redaelli**
Design and fabrication of GaN-based laser diodes for single-mode and narrow-linewidth applications
ISBN: 978-3-95404-586-0, 29,70 EUR, 176 Seiten

Band 29: **Martin Spreemann**
Resonatorkonzepte für Hochleistungs-Diodenlaser
mit ausgedehnten lateralen Dimensionen
ISBN: 978-3-95404-628-7, 25,15 EUR, 128 Seiten

Cuvillier Verlag
Internationaler wissenschaftlicher Fachverlag

Innovationen mit Mikrowellen und Licht
Forschungsberichte aus dem Ferdinand-Braun-Institut, Leibniz-Institut für Höchstfrequenztechnik

Herausgeber: Prof. Dr. G. Tränkle, Prof. Dr.-Ing. W. Heinrich

Band 30: **Christian Fiebig**
Diodenlaser mit Trapezstruktur und hoher Brillanz für die Realisierung einer Frequenzkonversion auf einer mikro-optischen Bank
ISBN: 978-3-95404-690-4, 26,30 EUR, 140 Seiten

Band 31: **Viola Küller**
Versetzungsreduzierte AlN- und AlGaN-Schichten als Basis für UV LEDs
ISBN: 978-3-95404-741-3, 34,40 EUR, 164 Seiten

Band 32: **Daniel Jedrzejczyk**
Efficient frequency doubling of near-infrared diode lasers using quasi phase-matched waveguides
ISBN: 978-3-95404-958-5, 27,90 EUR, 134 Seiten

Band 33: **Sylvia Hagedorn**
Hybrid-Gasphasenepitaxie zur Herstellung von Aluminiumgalliumnitrid
ISBN: 978-3-95404-985-1, 38,00 EUR, 176 Seiten

Band 34: **Alexander Kravets**
Advanced Silicon MMICs for mm-Wave Automotive Radar Front-Ends
ISBN: 978-3-95404-986-8, 31,90 EUR, 156 Seiten

Band 35: **David Feise**
Longitudinale Modenfilter für Kantenemitter im roten Spektralbereich
ISBN: 978-3-7369-9116-3, 39,20 EUR, 168 Seiten

Band 36: **Ksenia Nosaeva**
Indium phosphide HBT in thermally optimized periphery for applications up to 300GHZ
ISBN: 978-3-7369-287-0, 42,00 EUR, 154 Seiten

Band 37: **Muhammad Maruf Hossain**
Signal Generation for Millimeter Wave and THZ Applications in InP-DHBT and InP-on-BiCMOS Technologies
ISBN: 978-3-7369-9335-8, 35,60 EUR, 136 Seiten

Band 38: **Sirinpa Monayakul**
Development of Sub-mm Wave Flip-Chip Interconnect
ISBN: 978-3-7369-9410-2, 44,00 EUR, 146 Seiten

Band 39: **Moritz Brendel**
Charakterisierung und Optimierung von (Al, Ga) N-basierten UV-Photodetektoren
ISBN: 978-3-7369-9465-2, 49,90 EUR, 196 Seiten

Band 40: **Erdenetsetseg Luvsandamdin**
Development of micro-integrated diode lasers for precision quantum optics experiments in space
ISBN: 978-3-7369-9479-9, 39,00 EUR, 126 Seiten

Cuvillier Verlag
Internationaler wissenschaftlicher Fachverlag

Innovationen mit Mikrowellen und Licht
Forschungsberichte aus dem Ferdinand-Braun-Institut,
Leibniz-Institut für Höchstfrequenztechnik

Herausgeber: Prof. Dr. G. Tränkle, Prof. Dr.-Ing. W. Heinrich

Band 41: **Thi Nghiem Vu**
Development and analysis of diode laser ns-MOPA systems
for high peak power application
ISBN: 978-3-7369-9480-5, 38,80 EUR, 138 Seiten

Band 42: **Christian Bansleben**
Differentieller Mikrowellen-Leistungsoszillator für die Realisierung
ultrakompakter Plasmaquellen in Matrixanordnung
ISBN: 978-3-7369-9530-7, 34,90 EUR, 136 Seiten

Band 43: **Martin Winterfeldt**
Investigation of slow-axis beam quality degradation
in high-power broad area diode lasers
ISBN: 978-3-7369-9733-2, 39,90 EUR, 158 Seiten

Band 44: **Jonathan Decker**
Investigation of monolithically integrated spectral stabilization
in high-brightness broad area diode lasers
ISBN: 978-3-7369-9798-1, 49,50 EUR, 174 Seiten

Band 45: **Andreea Cristina Andrei**
Untersuchung und Optimierung robuster und hochlinearer
rauscharmer Verstärker in GaN-Technologie
ISBN: 978-3-7369-9810-0, 39,90 EUR, 148 Seiten

Band 46: **Peng Luo**
GaN HEMT Modeling Including Trapping Effects Based on
Chalmers Model and Pulsed S-Parameter Measurements
ISBN: 978-3-7369-9906-0, 48,00 EUR, 160 Seiten

Band 47: **Jörg Jeschke**
Entwicklung von optisch pumpbaren UVC-Lasern auf AlGaN-Basis
Chalmers Model and Pulsed S-Parameter Measurements
ISBN: 978-3-7369-9918-3, 44,90 EUR, 176 Seiten

www.ingramcontent.com/pod-product-compliance
Lightning Source LLC
Chambersburg PA
CBHW070831300426
44111CB00014B/2524